The Gift of Policewomen

The Gift of Policewomen

Robert N. Ullman

LINDA
ALL THE BEST
BOB ULLMAN

NUTCRACKER PUBLISHING
REDMOND, OREGON

The Gift of Policewomen

Printed in the United States.

Nutcracker Publishing
525 Nutcracker Drive
Redmond, OR 97756

Editing and Design by Indigo: Editing, Design, and More

ISBN: 978-0-578-40303-8
Library of Congress Control Number: 2018962079

For Madeline O'Loughlin Ullman, my five-year-old granddaughter,
who expresses a desire to help people and give back to others.

For Wilma Chandler Crounse, my grandmother,
who served as Lola Baldwin's assistant from 1909 to 1918,
when she retired to raise a daughter and become a leader in her community.

Contents

Preface

My motivation for writing *The Gift of Policewomen* came to me in 1965 following the funeral of my maternal grandmother, Wilma Pearl (Chandler) Crounse. Although my mother assured me that she had mentioned her mother's earlier years to me, I only remembered my grandmother as a small, gray-haired, elderly lady.

I had known Grandmother ("Grandma" was reserved for my other grandmother) as a very old woman. I did remember rare childhood visits to her home with my grandfather in Portland, Oregon, though. One of them occurred on my first Easter, when my mother took me to my grandmother's house. Everyone was dressed in their finest church clothes. Just as all of the adults were ready to get in the car, little Bobby started to cry. Grandmother quickly realized that I needed a change of clothing. As she removed my clothes, her newborn grandson showered his grandmother's new Easter bonnet. This was not my favorite memory of my grandmother, but the family recalled it with delight for years. My grandfather was an engaging, not to mention tall, man when standing next to his wife. Neal R. Crounse (whose first name is my middle name) worked at a law firm in downtown Portland, and on at least one occasion I was allowed to visit his workplace. In those early years, there had been several occasions when my sister and I were put on an airplane from Seattle, Washington, where we were loaded down with comic books (all of which we read before the plane took off) and turned over to a stewardess who took us to our seats and looked after us on our flight to Grandmother's house.

At Grandmother's funeral in 1965, though, other attendees had much different memories to share. I was shocked to learn that she had been a member of Portland Police Department's Women's Protective Division. These two images of my beloved grandmother—frail, loving, old woman and young, important policewoman—stood at odds in my mind, and I set out to research her earlier life and police work to know her better.

I learned that in mid-April 1907, halfway between the two major events that affected Portland's need for police help, Wilma Pearl Chandler graduated from Pacific University in Forest Grove, Oregon. The school

Portrait of Wilma Pearl Chandler. (Courtesy author's family archives.)

was located about thirty miles west of Portland and only two blocks from her house. Her path to graduation had been difficult.

Grandmother had been born in 1881 in The Dalles, a small farm community near the Columbia River and approximately eighty miles east of Portland. Her father made a living by hiring himself out to local farmers, and as jobs faded, he took his wife and daughter, Wilma Pearl, farther upriver in his quest for work. Another daughter, Helen, was born in the summer of 1885, when Wilma was just short of her fourth birthday and the family was living south of Pendleton.

Not long after that, Wilma's father's strength gave out due to years of hard work at harrowing, plowing, sowing wheat, planting potatoes, and more. Since the beginning of his marriage several years before, Willie had been documenting health problems in his diary:

> *Married, Sunday 12, 1882*
> *Wednesday 19, sowed wheat and harrowed. Cold and snowing.*
> *Thursday 20, Sick & Cold.*
> *Friday 21, Sick, rain and snow.*
> *Saturday 22, Sick, cold & a little snow.*

Sunday he was "Sick" but noted a letter from his brother Arthur and a card from his oldest sister, Julia Hill. Then the entry for Monday read simply, "Sick," followed by Tuesday, "chored, planted potatoes." He had a long history of illness and working in spite of it, but by 1885 it was becoming clear that his body could not hold up under those circumstances.

With a wife and two small daughters to support, Willie seemed to have found little time to attend to his own health. His mother, Persis Warren Chandler, lived in Forest Grove, two hundred miles to the west, and wrote a letter suggesting that Willie and his family return to her home. But Willie's second daughter was still an infant, and they worried about the toll the trip would take on her, so they waited until Helen was stronger before accepting his mother's proposal. In the fall of 1885, Willie B. Chandler and his family arrived at his parents' home in Washington County. Willie died there in early December 1885. Persis took in her two granddaughters, Wilma and Helen, along with the girls' widowed mother, Emma Chandler.

As it turned out, Willie came from a somewhat unfortunate family, and I imagined my grandmother growing up to learn of the family strife. Persis had lost her very first child. In 1872 Willie's father, Rev. George Clinton Crounse, was paralyzed while on a trip to preach in The Dalles. He was taken to his home in Forest Grove in a state of complete paralysis. Persis cared for him for the remainder of his life, from 1872 to January 1885. Her daughter Sarah married a farmer near Salem in 1867, only to watch her husband and all three of their children die in the early 1870s. Sarah returned home to live with her mother in Forest Grove.

By the Christmas of 1885, Persis Chandler found herself the head of a household of five including her widowed daughter Sarah, her widowed daughter-in-law Emma, and two young granddaughters, Wilma Pearl and Helen Willie, who were raised by the three older women. It was a house filled with females.

Wilma and Helen Chandler grew to adulthood both beloved, and each aware that she was expected to do her share. The sisters learned to read the Bible, help with chores, respect education, and gather food for the table. The family lived two blocks from Pacific University, and while many of their friends left school to find work or marry and have children, the Chandler girls had looked forward to the possibility of attending college since their early years.

Wilma Pearl chose to seek a four-year degree from Pacific, while Helen elected to obtain a teaching degree. Persis explained to her granddaughters that they would need help to achieve their goals but assured them that she would assist them as much as possible. Helen was able to finish her less expensive goal with minimal help, but it was necessary for Wilma to alternate between taking her college courses and dropping out of school periodically to work for her uncle in nearby McMinnville in order to complete her education.

Nevertheless, Grandmother Wilma was considered a leader at her university, frequently appearing in the *Oregonian* newspaper as a main contact for various events. She also played the piano, and during a competitive oratorical contest on February 8, 1901, she and a Miss Ora Caples played a piano duet of the *Spanische Tänze* by Moszkowski while the judges determined the winners of the Speaking Prizes.

As Portland's 1905 Lewis and Clark Centennial Exposition approached, Wilma saw a YWCA advertisement for young women, particularly college girls, to volunteer to help out at the Women's Building on the fairgrounds, and she decided to skip her 1905 term to do so. She would not be paid for volunteering, but the experience seemed worth it. During this volunteer stint, Wilma met Lola Baldwin, who at that time was heading the charge to protect young women coming to town for the exposition and advocating for safety

Chandler's passport photo for the 1905 Lewis and Clark Exposition. (Courtesy author's family archives.)

across the city. They worked together and became friends, and their paths would cross again—and make history—soon.

Eventually in my research, I would learn that Portland's exposition was a turning point for the city. Lola Baldwin's involvement in it, as well as the involvement of the many women like my grandmother she recruited, would spell one part of the beginning of the American policewomen movement. But at first, I was still focused on my grandmother—the exposition and Lola Baldwin were curiosities to expand upon at a later date.

And so Wilma Pearl Chandler, who had begun as a member of the class of 1904, due to her slow road to a diploma, finally graduated from Pacific University three years later as a member of the class of 1907. All women at Pacific were automatically members of the YWCA. As such, and probably due in part to her experience volunteering with the organization during the exposition, she developed a longing to work with the YWCA in Portland, a goal she might not have achieved had she graduated earlier, due to the organization's structural changes just before that. Wilma Pearl was hired in the first week of January 1908 to fill the role of membership chair and turned out to be very successful at it.

Wilma was assigned a desk in the business room and soon renewed her friendship with Lola Baldwin. At about the same time, Wilma renamed herself Pearl Chandler, and she was soon acknowledged by other YWCA leaders for her success in improving membership. Pearl was now twenty-six years old and one of the 3 percent nationally of women who held a four-year college degree. She had struggled long and hard to achieve this goal and looked forward to continuing to contribute to society.

Over the next couple of years, the YWCA's funding and role in the protection of Portland's youth went through transitions, eventually leading to the launch of the Women's Protective Division. In 1909 Pearl Chandler was hired as assistant superintendent to Superintendent Lola G. Baldwin, and they worked together until 1918.

Various articles appear in the *Oregonian* featuring my grandmother's public safety work, particularly her role in finding lost children, caring for the mentally ill, judging modesty, and advocating for women's groups during this time. Of course, her wedding to my grandfather was a focal point for the community and papers as well. The articles I found most interesting include:

Lost Kelso Girl Is Found: Freda Lyon, 16 Years Old, Is Domestic in St. Helen's Hall

The Morning Oregonian, September 14, 1911

Working as a domestic in St. Helen's Hall, a finishing school for girls, while her parents and the police were searching high and low for her, Freda Lyon, the 16-year-old girl who left Chehalis, September 6, supposedly for Kelso, her home, was found by Miss Wilma Pearl Chandler, assistant in the Department of Public Safety for Women, last night on advices received from several different sources.

The girl told Miss Chandler that family differences led her to leave her home. She had a good position at St. Helen's Hall when found, and had not been under the influence of suspected persons, as her parents charged when they raised the alarm concerning her disappearance.

As the result of newspaper publicity during her absence, many calls to the Department of Public Safety were answered and several other girls answering Miss Lyon's general description are expected to be found as a result of clews sent in. ❧

Society News

By Gertrude P. Corbett

The Morning Oregonian, January 7, 1915

Of interest yesterday was the wedding of Miss Wilma Pearl Chandler and Neal Remington Crounse, which was solemnized at the home of the bride's mother, Mrs. Emma Wooley Chandler. Dr. Leonard W. Riley, president of the McMinnville College, officiated.

The Wedding was a charming though simple affair, and the house was decorated prettily for the occasion. Miss Helen Chandler, sister of the bride, was her only attendant, and Dr. J. Harvey Johnson acted as best man. The bride was charming in a handsome robe of ivory-tined crepe de chine, embellished with rare lace. Her full-length filmy veil was wreathed with orange

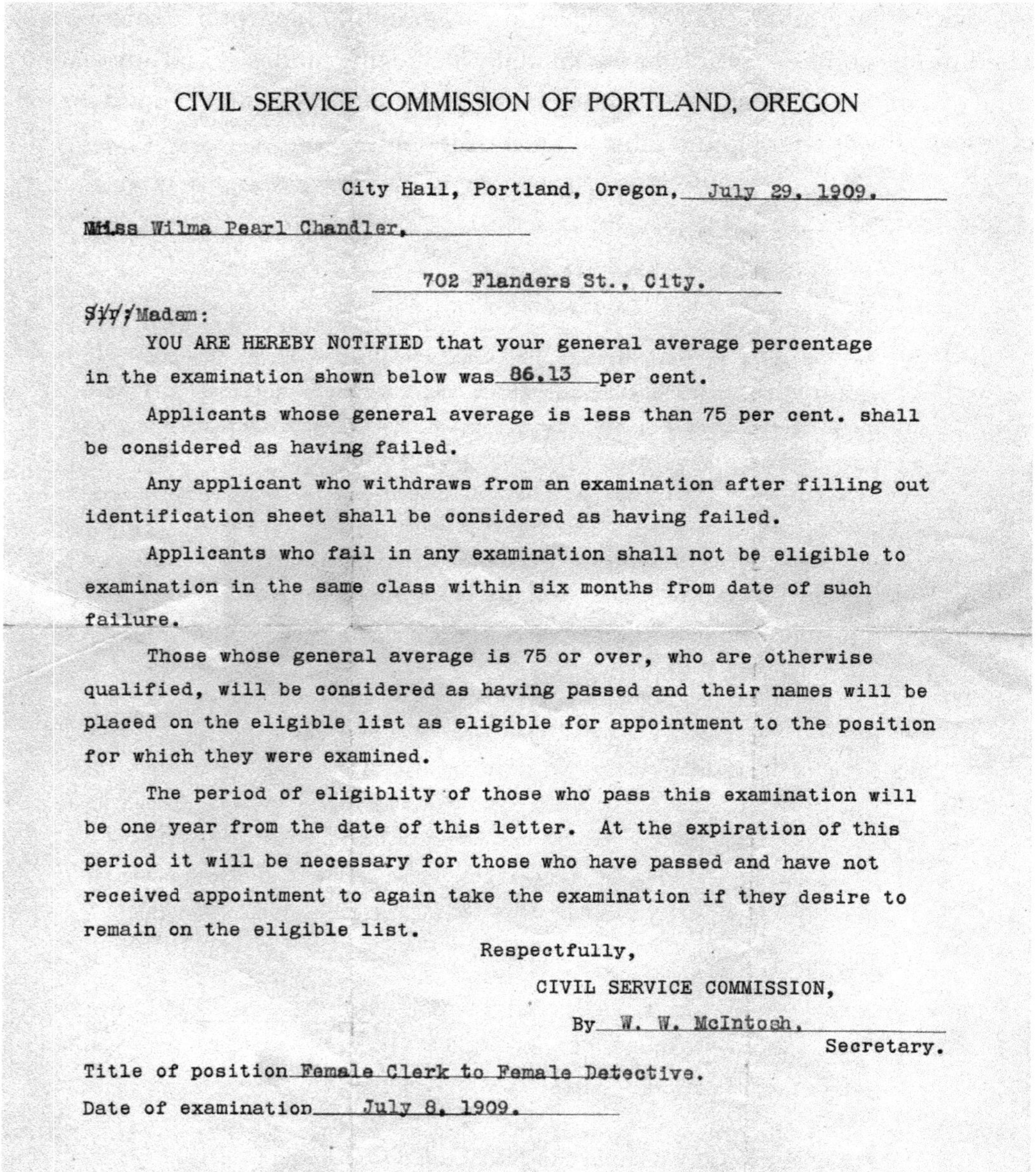

CIVIL SERVICE COMMISSION OF PORTLAND, OREGON

City Hall, Portland, Oregon, July 29, 1909.

Miss Wilma Pearl Chandler,

702 Flanders St., City.

~~Sir;~~Madam:

YOU ARE HEREBY NOTIFIED that your general average percentage in the examination shown below was 86.13 per cent.

Applicants whose general average is less than 75 per cent. shall be considered as having failed.

Any applicant who withdraws from an examination after filling out identification sheet shall be considered as having failed.

Applicants who fail in any examination shall not be eligible to examination in the same class within six months from date of such failure.

Those whose general average is 75 or over, who are otherwise qualified, will be considered as having passed and their names will be placed on the eligible list as eligible for appointment to the position for which they were examined.

The period of eligiblity of those who pass this examination will be one year from the date of this letter. At the expiration of this period it will be necessary for those who have passed and have not received appointment to again take the examination if they desire to remain on the eligible list.

Respectfully,

CIVIL SERVICE COMMISSION,

By W. W. McIntosh,

Secretary.

Title of position Female Clerk to Female Detective.

Date of examination July 8, 1909.

Letter informing Chandler that she had passed her civil service exam, with her position noted as female detective. (Courtesy author's family archives.)

blossoms and her only jewels were a handsome platinum necklace and lavaliere of diamonds and pearls, the gift of the bridegroom. She also carried a shower bouquet of bride roses and lilies of the valley....

Mr. and Mrs. Crounse left for a short wedding trip and upon their return will be at home in the Mayo apartments.

Mr. Crounse is assistant clerk of the Municipal Court and his bride is assistant to Mrs. Lola G. Baldwin in the department of public safety for young women. ❧

PHONES: MAIN 7181
A 6751

SECOND AND OAK

DEPARTMENT OF PUBLIC SAFETY
WOMEN'S PROTECTIVE DIVISION

MISS W. P. CHANDLER,
ASST. SUPT.

Wilma Pearl Chandler's business card. (Courtesy author's family archives.)

Bathing Suits Worn by Girls Approved: Censors Find One Abbreviated Costume Too Immodest, but Mermaid Ignores Plea: Moral Effects Studied.

The Morning Oregonian, June 30, 1915

Swimming Resorts on River Visited and Dwindling Apparel Is Noted. Only Law Provides Men Wear Trunks in Certain Limits.

"Passed by the board of censorship."

This applies to river bathing resorts visited yesterday by seven representatives of Mayor Albee, to whom had come a letter of protest against abbreviated bathing suites used by girl swimmers last year.

Mrs. Sarah A. Evans, president of the Oregon Federation of Women's Clubs; Mrs. Wilma C. Crounse, of the police protective bureau for women; Captain J. Speier, harbormaster, and four newspaper men, one each from the Portland dailies, made up the group of censors.

Only One Costume Criticised.

One girl's costume only was seen that was thought to be stingy, and a number of the censors did not object to that. However, it was worn by a young water nymph outside of the swimming resorts and could not be charged to them.

It was a long, black tights suit, such as is worn by stage swimmers, and the girl appeared to have been melted and poured into it. With three other girls in abbreviated costumes, she was swimming off a houseboat, and the party came across the river in a launch to have their pictures taken.

The girls were having a frolic by themselves, with a boatman along to run their launch, and to the majority of the investigating party, the picture of these mermaids disporting themselves in the water was a charming one. The tightly clinging black suit, innocent of a skirt, was, however, declared by two members to both immodest and immoral....

Men's swimming suits worn at both the Oaks and Windemuth came in for criticism at the hands of Mrs. Crounse, although no complaint has been received at the City Hall on this subject.

"I think immodesty is shown by these suits, they are so much abbreviated," she said. "Many of the men swimmers should be compelled to wear more clothing. It isn't fair to pick on the girls when boys and men are allowed to wear such suits."...

The two women censors did not object to bare limbs for girl swimmers, about half those seen yesterday dispensing with stockings while in the water....

It seems the work of both my grandparents was commonly a favorite topic with the Portland media, and reporters liked to have some fun with them as well, as is seen in this article:

Fair Auto Driver's Traffic Signal Misses Its Mark.

The Morning Oregonian, October 7, 1915

Young Man Responds to Inviting Gesture at Turn and Grasps Hand but Finds His Wife.

When, in obedience to traffic rules, the fair woman autoist extends her hand in a signal to those behind that she is about to turn a corner, it is an inviting gesture to the young man standing on the curbing, if not properly done. Therefore, so, and because of which the wave should be business-like and brief, and not the dainty, leisurely gesture of one about to shake the hand of a dear friend.

Passers-by at Fifth and Morrison streets yesterday were hugely amused, when a young man stepped to the side of a passing automobile and cordially grasped the white hand of a young woman as it gracefully waved the signal to automobiles following.

"Pleased tuh meetcha," spoke he.

"Oh," said she, a vivid red dyeing her cheeks, as she turned indignantly upon the impertinent person.

No, kind reader, he was not one who had lingered too long near the flowing bowl, nor a masher of the Nth degree of boldness. He was the husband of the woman. It was a neat little surprise.

Neal R. Crounse, Deputy City Clerk, noticed his wife, Wilma Chandler Crounse, acting superintendent of the Bureau of Municipal Protection for Women, with Miss Martha Randall, assistant superintendent, rounding the corner at Fifth and Morrison as he was returning from lunch and thought it a good—and safe—opportunity to accept the invitation so often extended unthinkingly, by women autoists. ❧

The newspapers also often reported that my grandmother would be making presentations to advocate for resources for women, as shown in these 1915 and 1916 excerpts:

> At the vesper service of the Young Women's Christian Association on Sunday at 4:30 o'clock Mrs. Wilma Chandler Crounse will tell all about the Big Sisterhood and will make a plea for more members.... All young women strangers in the city are invited. A social hour will follow the programme.

> Wednesday morning, December 20, the Coterie will enjoy the following programme...Mrs. Wilma Chandler Crounse will talk on "The Need for a Woman's

SLY CUPID INVADES POLICE HEADQUARTERS

Romance flourishes even in the gray corridors of Police Headquarters. Neil R. Crounse, assistant clerk of the Municipal Court, and Miss Wilma Pearl Chandler, assistant superintendent and probation officer of the Department of Public Safety for Young Girls, were married this afternoon at the home of the bride's mother, Mrs. Emma W. Chandler, 452 East Tenth street North. The news surprised all but their intimate friends. When neither bride nor bridegroom appeared for duty this morning the secret was out.

The Rev. Leonard W. Riley, president of McMinnville College, who baptized the bride, officiated, and Miss Helen W. Chandler, sister of the bride, was bridesmaid. Dr. J. Harvey Johnson attended the groom and only a very few of the immediate relatives and friends of the two families were present.

Shortly after noon today, Crounse, accompanied by Dr. Johnson, applied for a marriage license and after giving the necessary statistics, hurried away in an automobile.

Both bride and groom are widely known throughout the state, Crounse having served as court clerk since October 1, 1911, when he was appointed

there she organized among the employes of Olds, Wortman & King Alpha Delta Society, an organization that was started to aid the ...

Wilma Pearl Chandler's wedding announcement.

Detention Home," and Mrs. C. M. Kiggins is to give one of her inimitable readings, "Christmas in the Quarters."

One of the last features the *Oregonian* ran on my grandmother perhaps best shows her feminist nature and skill at police work:

Woman Is Good Shot: Mrs. Wilma Crounse Shows Policemen How to Use Revolvers
The Morning Oregonian, January 24, 1918

Mrs. Wilma Pearl Crounse is a "lioness" in police circles today, for yesterday afternoon she descended into the basement at the central station, slammed away with a revolver at 10 yards and hit the target 10 times with 10 shots.

Mrs. Crounse made a record of 63 out of a possible 100, thereby placing her in the class with the best 10 shots among the officers and men of the bureau. This, too, was her first trial with a revolver, although she is a good shot with a rifle.

From researching Grandmother Crounse, my interest in this project grew to explore the life and career of her friend and supervisor Lola Baldwin and then other pioneering policewomen Alice Stebbins Wells and Marie Connolly Owens. As time passed, I learned that most other books about the history of police provide only brief glimpses at policewomen. I became increasingly convinced that my book should become larger than I had envisioned when I began. I moved from writing a nice little memento for my late grandmother and expanded the work into a more detailed study of Portland's policewomen, and eventually into a more comprehensive history of policewomen in America and beyond.

I enjoyed reading newspaper, journal, and internet articles on the many stages of the policewomen movement. This book is a compilation of the research that started with my grandmother and led to a twenty-year project. It covers the origins of police, the earliest policewomen, how women in police forces became a movement, and how it's changed over the past 125 years. It also takes a look at the modern police crisis related to excessive force and the challenges that today's policewomen face as they still make up only 12 percent of American law enforcement. Other countries are emphasizing the value of policewomen as well, as will be seen in the final chapter.

While I would love to publish a comprehensive volume that chronicles every original source in the policewomen movement, the size would be unwieldy. The articles and book excerpts that are featured in this book have been curated to reduce length and redundancy, with the hope that the compilation provides readers with an accurate picture of the policewomen movement from its inception to today. I have enjoyed the journey and hope my readers will feel the same.

—Robert N. Ullman
Redmond, Oregon
May 2018

Chapter 1
From Police Origins to Policewoman Pioneers

The *American College Dictionary* defines an *oversight* as a "failure to notice or consider." The history of women police in the United States and elsewhere is often written as if not much of importance happened until the 1970s.

The period ranging from 1893 to the 1920s was a time that brought forth the earliest women police in the United States and Europe. Marie Connolly Owens, Lola Greene Baldwin, Alice Stebbins Wells, and the numerous others who followed them at the turn of the century broke new ground for women. The "rules" were not yet set. Owens and Baldwin chose not to wear uniforms—so did Wells in her first few years. All three were pioneers in their field who have largely been dismissed by modern history writers. But the policewomen movement continued to grow, despite major challenges during the Depression when jobs were scarce and in the post-WWII era when women were expected to return to their roles as housewives, through the women's movement surge of the seventies, and into the past few decades and the various challenges policewomen face in their bureaus today.

While there are some brief biographies of the founders of the policewomen movement, the full impact of their contributions and the many women who worked with them and in the decades following have been largely overlooked. *The Gift of Policewomen* endeavors to fill this gap by presenting a curated compilation of articles and other original sources to provide an overall picture of the policewomen movement with some editorial context where necessary. Original sources are indicated by the title and author's name (if available) appearing first and the quoted text thereafter. They are transcribed to reflect the original sources, meaning you'll likely see some spelling, capitalization, and formatting variants to reflect the time and the original author's or publication's style. All reprinted materials have been included with permission from the original author or publisher, or they are under public domain or fair use copyright laws. Please see the bibliography and special credits page in the back of the book for more information.

Before we launch into the specific stories of policewomen, it's important to understand the history of police, how they came to be a part of society, and how the concept of policing has changed over time.

The History of Police

Police: History

Encyclopedia of Crime and Justice

Throughout the history of civilization, societies have sought protection for their members and possessions. In early civilizations, members of one's family provided this protection. Richard Lundman has suggested that the development of formal policing resulted from a process of three developmental stages. The first stage involves *informal policing,* where all members of a society share equally in the responsibility for providing protection and keeping order. The second stage, *transitional policing,* occurs when police functions are informally assigned to particular members of the society. This stage serves as a transition into *formal policing,* where specific members of the community assume formal responsibility for protection and social control. Lundman suggests that the history of police involved a shift from informal to formal policing. Indeed, as societies have evolved from *mechanical* (members share similar beliefs and values but meet their basic needs independently) to *organic* (members are dependent upon one another as a result of specialization) societies, social control became more complex. Whereas there was little need for formal, specialized policing in mechanical societies, organic societies require more specialization to ensure public order.

Over time, organic societies developed into states and governments. A *state* is defined as "a political creation that has the recognized authority to use and maintain a monopoly on the use of force within a clearly defined jurisdiction," while a *government* is a "political institution of the state that uses organization, bureaucracy, and formality to regulate social interactions." The origins of formal policing began with the organization of societies into states and governments.

The form of government heavily influences the structure of police organizations... [and] "the source of state power ultimately represents the basis of police authority as well." Different forms of government have established different types of police forces.... There are four different models of policing (i.e., communist, Anglo-Saxon, continental, and colonial) that differ based on their sources of legitimacy, organizational structure, and police function.... The communist model of policing obtains legitimacy through the communist political party, is organized as a centralized, armed militarized force, and performs the functions of crime control and enforcement of state ideology. The continental and colonial models have similar organizational structures and functions as the communist model, however the continental model obtains its legitimacy through the central government while the colonial model establishes legitimacy through the colonial authority. In comparison, the Anglo-Saxon model obtains legitimacy through local governments and is based in law. This model is organized as a decentralized force that is armed in some countries (United States) and not in others (England). Finally, police functions in this model include crime control, order maintenance, and welfare and administrative responsibilities. ❧

Sir Robert Peel, author of the most commonly used principles of law enforcement. (George Newenham Wright. Monograph. *Lancashire: Its History, Legends, and Manufactures.* London: Fisher, Son & Co., 183. Engraving by H. Robinson.)

As the above article intimates, fifteen centuries ago there were no policewomen. There were no policemen either. There were, however, European armies designed to protect one society against another. But when armies were victorious in their efforts, they were often allowed to turn upon the opposing army's peasants for ransacking, raping, and destruction. Sometimes they attacked their own peasants. In short, armies were not trustworthy police.

As the centuries passed and philosophers began to study the rights of man, they encouraged their societies toward more local forms of protective enforcement and away from uncontrollable troops. Early in the nineteenth century, a British statesman named Robert Peel set forth nine Principles of Law Enforcement. These were groundbreaking in that they infused police work with the ethics of public safety rather than enforcing military power over others. They were adopted by police departments throughout England and spread to other parts of the world. Even today, many police departments in both England and America post Peel's Principles on their websites.

Sir Robert Peel's Principles of Law Enforcement
1829

1. The basic mission for which police exist is to prevent crime and disorder as an alternative to the repression of crime and disorder by military force and severity of legal punishment.
2. The ability of the police to perform their duties is dependent upon *public approval* of police existence, actions, behavior and the ability of the police to secure and maintain *public respect.*
3. The police must secure the willing cooperation of the public in voluntary observance of the law to be able to secure and maintain public respect.
4. The degree of cooperation of the public that can be secured diminishes, proportionately, to the use of physical force and compulsion in achieving police objectives.
5. The police seek and preserve public favor, not by catering to public opinion, but by constantly demonstrating absolutely impartial service to the law, in complete independence of policy, and without regard to the justice or injustice of the substance of individual laws; by ready offering of individual service and friendship to all members of society without regard to their race or social standing[;] by ready exercise of individual laws and friendly good humor; and by ready offering of individual sacrifice in protecting and preserving life.
6. The police should use physical force to the extent necessary to secure observance of the law or to restore order only when the exercise of *persuasion, advice and warning* is found to be insufficient to achieve police objectives; and police should use only the minimum degree of physical force which is necessary on any particular occasion for achieving a police objective.
7. The police at all times should maintain a relationship with the public that gives reality to the historic tradition that *the police are the public* and *the public are the police*; the police are the only members of the public who are paid to give full-time attention to duties which are incumbent on every citizen in the intent of the community welfare.
8. The police should always direct their actions toward their functions and never appear to usurp the powers of the judiciary by avenging individuals or the state, or authoritatively judging guilt or punishing the guilty.

9. The test of police efficiency is the *absence* of crime and disorder, not the *visible evidence* of police action in dealing with them.

With these principles laid forth, clear parameters for the police profession and public safety officers were set. It was considered a career just for men, however, until the first policewomen would enter the scene nearly a century later.

Earliest Female Police

The earliest women to be involved in police work were known as matrons or police matrons. Their duties varied from state to state, county to county, and city to city. For the most part they were to visit women in jail and to stand by them in court when needed. However, there were dissimilarities from place to place. According to historian Lawrence C. Dame, the first American matrons were appointed in 1845 when "the American Female Reform Society secured the appointment of six women matrons in New York City—two at the City Prison (the Tombs) and four on Blackwell's Island—They were the first prison matrons in the United States."

During the 1870s, solely from a sense of civic duty, prominent women in Portland, Maine, visited incarcerated female prisoners and attended court with them when called on. During this period, women were detained in the same cells as men, and there was concern for their safety. In 1877 the city appointed one such visitor, Mrs. Mary J. Raymond, at the recommendation of the Women's Christian Temperance Union. She was named a police matron, and it was agreed that half of her salary that year would be paid by the city. In the following year her full salary was paid by the city. Mrs. Raymond's work primarily engaged her in responding to the large numbers of arrests in Maine for intoxication. She only served a few years, but it's estimated that she worked with approximately three hundred incarcerated women each year.

Maine's practice of placing men and women in the same cell was at last deemed indecent in 1894, which led to the building of separate cells exclusively for women beginning in 1899. Maine did not have a full-time policewoman until May 23, 1921, when Miss Elizabeth McDonough, a police department clerk for six years, was hired as a special patrol. She followed in her mother's footsteps—Mrs. Mary McDonough had been a police matron since 1917. Another mother-daughter pair, Lucy Grey and Aletha Gilbert, worked in Los Angeles as well.

An early matron in St. Paul, Minnesota, Miss Theresa Walsh was Irish and immigrated with her parents in 1851 at the age of fifteen. According to the Saint Paul Police Historical Society, "She received her

Lucy Grey, left, and her mother, Aletha Gilbert, both police matrons in Los Angeles. (Courtesy Los Angeles Police Museum.)

appointment as matron in April of 1896. A report of the city comptroller indicates Miss Walsh's salary at that time was $30 a month, less than half the wages of a patrolman conducting similar duties."

The interest in employing women in jails, courtrooms, and police departments continued, and by 1925 there were women employed as matrons and policewomen around the country and beyond. While these early police matrons opened the police department doors for women to hold positions, their duties were limited. Cities still relied on men to do official police work—that is, until three groundbreaking women began to work as police in three different parts of the country at nearly the same time.

The First Three American Policewomen

Marie Connolly Owens, Lola Greene Baldwin, and Alice Stebbins Wells are now widely recognized as the first American policewomen. They worked in Chicago, Illinois; Portland, Oregon; and Los Angeles, California, respectively, in the late 1800s and early 1900s. At the turn of the twentieth century, though, no one could have known the great impact they would have on police history.

Sergeant Marie Connolly Owens

While Sergeant Marie Connolly Owens's work with the police department in Chicago appears first in the timeline of policewomen, she was not recorded in the history books as such until 2010, when researcher Rick Barrett was looking into the history of Chicago law enforcement and found her records dating back to the 1890s, predating the previous claims that Lola Baldwin and Alice Stebbins Wells were the first American policewomen in 1908 and 1910, respectively. These records provided clear proof that Marie Connolly Owens was the true owner of that title.

Portrait of Marie Connolly Owens of the Chicago police force. (*Chicago Sun Tribune*, October 28, 1906.)

As journalist James Chung reported in *Hello Vancity* in 2010, Barrett's research revealed that Chicago had been facing a high degree of child exploitation in the late 1880s and in response: "The city agreed to hire five women to work as factory and tenement inspectors at a salary of $50 a month. Owens clinched one of the spots in 1889, beating out hundreds of applicants. Impressed by her work, the police force seconded her to its detective bureau in 1891."

Owens had been born Marie Connolly in 1853 in Ottawa, Canada. At age twenty-six, she married Thomas A. Owens, and the couple moved to Chicago for his job as a gas fitter. Sadly, Thomas died of typhoid fever in 1888, and Marie became a single mother and sole provider for her five young children. Surely child safety was as high in her mind as earning a paycheck.

Marie Owens took her job seriously and soon gained a reputation for effectively implementing the 1891 ordinance regarding child labor. As time passed she found herself helping not only children but also their families. It did not take long for Owens to learn that many families were suffering because their breadwinner had deserted them. She witnessed firsthand the many children forced to seek employment in order to keep their families from starving, so Owens became an expert at tracking down "wife deserters." A reform-minded new chief of police in Chicago became impressed with the fact that in addition to Marie's job, she was also assisting families and bringing delinquent husbands to justice. He offered to move her to the detective bureau of the police department, where Marie was awarded the rank of sergeant. With

THE ONLY WOMAN POLICE SERGEANT IN THE WORLD

"Sergeant No. 97," an Efficient Officer Whose Smile Makes Offenders Obey the Law.

Enforced Child Labor Law

Wins by Her Smile.

Laws Prevent Another Woman Sergeant.

Acts as Court of Final Resort.

Seldom Resorts to Force.

Appeals by Working Girls

Early evidence of Owens's status as the first policewoman. (*Chicago Sun Tribune*, August 7, 1904.)

her new badge, Owens became known as Sergeant No. 97. In addition to salary and a badge, she now also had arrest powers, which had previously only been granted to male detectives.

Because there had never been a female detective in Chicago, the usual forms used to hire and promote male police in 1893 were applied instead. Consequently, Sergeant Owens's paperwork listed the new sergeant as a "policeman." Hers was no small undertaking, and the work faced by the board of sanitary inspectors was revealed when "the United States Census of 1890 revealed that 1.5 million children between the ages of ten and fifteen were employed; nearly 20 percent of all children in that age range."

Marie fully understood what it meant to be in need, and this motivated her to help as many people as she could. In addition to locating delinquent dads, she worked tirelessly to help the poor, focusing especially on women and children. Before long she had widened her area of interests. She established schools within department stores so young working boys could be educated. She lobbied and won shorter workdays for young employees. When called upon by a family in distress, Owens at times gave money from her own pay to help the family.

In 1901 she wrote an article published in the *Chicago Tribune* detailing her work as a policewoman and the betterment of the community as a result:

Enforcement of the Child Labor Law: Twelve Years Detective Sergeant Detailed to Board of Education on This Work

By Mrs. Marie Owens

Chicago Tribune, 1901

For years there has stood upon the statute books of the State of Illinois law regarding the employment of children tender aged in the factories and workshops of this State. For some time after the passage of this law its enforcement was lax, there was no one detailed specially for the work, and the result was that the statute was almost flagrantly violated throughout Chicago. Under Mayor Washburne I was assigned to the Board of Education to enforce the compulsory education law and the law regarding the employment of children of ages less than 14 years. Previous to that time I was one of the five women sanitary inspectors working out of the Health office.

From time to time the Board of Education received letters telling of pitiable cases where children were compelled to work long hours to provide food for crippled mothers and fathers. Many of these cases were turned over to me. In the course of time the complaints increased at such an alarming rate that I was not able to do both the work of sanitary inspector and enforce the child labor law. Eventually I was transferred to the Board of Education and made the work of child labor and truancy, as well as compulsory education, my sole field.

The sights to be seen in the slums today can in no way compare with those of ten years ago and the suffering due to the inability of the older members of the family to work is, indeed, pitiable. Children were found working in factories all over the city, the frail little things in many cases being under 7. The pittance of 75 cents or $1 a week, however, helped to buy food for a sick mother, though it was at the cost of health and education.

When the work was first begun a woman wearing a police sergeant's star was a novelty. Manufacturers in some cases were not inclined to admit me to their workshops, but armed with the strong arm of the law and the will to do good I soon found that in most cases the merchants met me half way and rendered me great assistance. As a result the children were gradually thinned out, and the employers became accustomed to asking for affidavits required by law before work was given to children. Mothers had to depose as to the children's ages, and with these papers the latter were enabled to get employment in the larger factories and stores.

The good feeling promoted at the start of my work helped me immensely, and I can safely say that thousands of children were taken from work and sent to school without my knowledge. The manufacturer and shopkeeper took the law to heart and the children of tender age were rapidly taken from work and given a chance to learn. I have been doing the work for the Board of Education now for ten years and have never met any trouble owing to the changes of administration. All the superiors under whom I have worked have been most kind to me, and this treatment could but work to good advantage in discharging the duties of special officer for the board. Unpleasant features which were met with at the start have been eliminated, and the law is now as thoroughly obeyed as any on the statutes. ❧

In 1895 Chicago revised its civil service rules requiring all officers to pass the civil service examination. Marie scored a 99 percent, but she was not added to the civil service rolls until 1898, three years after she passed the exam and seven years after she joined the police force. Even after that, her position and the idea that there could be other policewomen remained contentious. In 1904 the *Chicago Daily Tribune* noted that the new rules "will forever prevent the appointment of more feminine patrolmen. Mrs. Owens will undoubtedly remain as she has been for fifteen years, the only woman police officer in the world."

In 1906 the *Chicago Daily Tribune* noted that Sergeant Owens "has lost none of her womanly attributes and other detectives in the central office lift their hats when they chance to meet her." She stated her own self-evaluation: "I like to do police work.... It gives me a chance to help women and children who need help. Of course I know little about the kind of work the men do. I never go out looking for robbers or highwaymen." At this point Marie Owens had been a policewoman for thirteen years but was mostly uncelebrated outside of Chicago. She retired in 1923. Chicago's first ten official policewomen were hired in 1913, no doubt in part due to the path blazed for them by Owens.

Through thirty years of service, Marie Connolly Owens remained on the police rolls in Chicago—but always as a "patrolman." Her job was not solely gender-specific: she brought in men who had deserted their wives and children and therefore dealt with fathers, mothers, and their children. It is difficult to imagine that in the course of her thirty-year career as a "policeman," no one thought to acknowledge her actual gender.

Superintendent Lola Greene Baldwin

Lola Baldwin holds a special place of importance for me, personally. My initial interest in researching policewomen stemmed from learning my own grandmother, Wilma Pearl Chandler Crounse, had served on the Women's Protective Division with the Portland Police Department in Oregon—a bureau that Lola Greene Baldwin started. For a long time, my research on this project centered around Grandmother Crounse, as I detailed in the preface, as well as Lola Baldwin and the 1905 Lewis and Clark Centennial Exposition.

Lola was born Aurora Greene in 1860 in New York, grew up in Rochester, was nicknamed Lola, and was a teacher in the area. In 1880 she moved to Lincoln, Nebraska, to pursue teaching work, and in 1884 she married LeGrand Baldwin, who was a dry goods merchant and moved his family through several cities for his work. The couple had two sons. In most towns where they lived, Lola volunteered with the city to help wayward girls, including serving on the boards for two branches of the girls refuge Florence Crittenton Homes. LeGrand was relocated yet again in 1904, this time to Portland, Oregon, not long before the nation's next grand fair would be held there.

The 1905 Lewis and Clark Centennial Exposition was initially planned to be simply a centennial celebration, but the exposition's title was eventually morphed awkwardly to become the Lewis and Clark Centennial Exposition *and* American Pacific Exposition *and* Oriental Fair. In a short four and a half months, the event would attract approximately 1,588,000 visitors.

Having seen the headlines from previous World's Fairs, city leaders knew they needed someone to protect the many women and girls who were about to descend on Portland. These young women were expecting to find food, housing, and jobs galore, though they had no idea that not nearly enough resources existed for them all. In addition, prostitutes, swindlers, pickpockets, thieves, and others arrived early looking to take advantage of the innocent. The Travelers Aid Society (TAS) was designed to assist visitors in need. Others of the city's charities involved in the mission included the YWCA, Florence Crittenton Home, General Federation of Women's Clubs, Portland Woman's Club, Portland Women's Union, Oregon Social Hygiene Society, and religious institutions.

The task force was outspoken about its mission, and many newspaper articles were published about it.

Protection of Girls Object of Society

The Oregon Daily Journal, March 7, 1905

The finance committee of the Portland Travelers' Aid association has issued a call for the membership dues of the various organisations belonging to the association, as there is an immediate need of funds to begin the work planned. The society is for the purpose of protecting girls. The international exposition travelers' aid committee has telegraphed that they have reconvened to help the Lewis and Clark workers and wish to know local plans. Individuals interested in the work may identify themselves with the society by the payment of individual dues at the Y. W. C. A. office, Sixth and Oak streets.

Rev. E. B. Uts of Spokane has sent to the association a letter which shows the need of independent local work on the part of the society.

Lola Baldwin and her husband, LeGrand, had just arrived in Portland after his transfer from the East. Although she had promised her husband that she would help him with setting up his office, she was eager to put her experience working for girls' protection to work. She contacted the local Florence Crittenton Home and was quickly added to the board. Recognizing the value of an experienced woman such as Baldwin, the board established work for her in the north end, an area notorious for its prostitution. Lola quickly arranged to meet with women who required medical help. She also began visiting the madams of Portland's bordellos to get acquainted and to request that since young women were already arriving in Portland and finding themselves in trouble, the madams notify Lola of those who were underage or were not suited for the business. For the most part she found the madams to be cooperative.

Jessie Honeyman, president of the YWCA, approached Baldwin to get acquainted and was impressed with her experience. Honeyman had written a letter to the national office in New York requesting assistance from someone with experience at World's Fairs but found that most New Yorkers were not available. Honeyman recruited Baldwin to be the secretary of the YWCA's Travelers Aid Society as the city prepared for the exposition and endeavored to keep women and girls safe until it was over. Although Lola Baldwin's work in Portland was not considered police work at first, it related directly to public safety and would eventually define her duties as a policewoman.

Women of the Travelers Aid Society, including Lola Baldwin at center. (Oregon Historical Society, #bb017352.)

Lola had a large and competent corps of volunteers. She borrowed from her own vast experiences preventing crime in the East and Midwest and created a new focus in the policing of Portland's World's Fair. Unlike safety officers of other recent fairs, she befriended both Portland's underworld environment as well as its civic leaders and called on both elements to help control fairgoers and businesses. She induced both elements to attend to the protection of young women and girls. Her own Travelers Aid work would be staffed by women volunteers, primarily recruited from nearby colleges and universities, rather than salaried men as other fairs had done. Baldwin's volunteers wore plain clothes along with large and easily identifiable ribbons as opposed to the uniforms and swords that had been seen at Chicago's 1893 fair.

It may have been an article like the one following that enticed my grandmother Wilma Pearl Chandler (later policewoman Wilma Crounse) to join the crews of college women who would help protect girls coming to Portland for the fair.

College Girls Will Serve in This Hotel

The Oregon Daily Journal, April 23, 1905

The Young Women's Christian association of Portland is making preparations for the comfort of many visitors to the Lewis and Clark exposition this summer. The building in process of erection immediately northeast of the Liberal Arts will...furnish all the conveniences of a home for women. A large dining-room, rest rooms, lavatories and bath, hospital room, children's nursery, information bureau and check room will be included in the conveniences offered. The idea is to make the building as homelike as possible, that it may emphasize that for which the association pre-eminently stands—home comforts for women. All the assistants in the building will be college girls taken from the associations of Oregon colleges. The waitresses, maids in attendance and clerks will all be educated and cultured girls who will be pleasant to meet. It is the hope of the association to give some entertainment in the building every week, of musical, literary or social interest, to promote the social feeling among the visitors. Letters of inquiry are received every day from all over the states about the fair and what accommodations will be offered by the association.

Impressed with how well Baldwin had summed up the situation in less than two months and was prepared to address needed remedies, the TAS leaders promoted her from distribution secretary to superintendent of the their exposition effort. This took place just prior to a critical May 20 meeting of the TAS at which the group discussed whether to accept the offer of the New York Travelers Aid to send two of their leaders to head Portland's operation. To the great relief of the Portland women, Baldwin was showing herself clearly up to the task of dealing with such surprises, and with the fair's June 1 opening rapidly approaching, it was agreed that there was really no time available to spend looking for a different leader.

It surprised some that Baldwin was taking on the job of superintendent of the Travelers Aid Society so soon after having arrived in Portland. The reason for the rush was that Portland's women had only recently come to understand the potential dangers to women and young girls who were beginning to arrive for the Lewis and Clark Centennial. Lola's husband and two children had arrived with her, and it was clear that Mrs. Baldwin had no intention of leaving the city anytime soon. Lola was chosen based on her twenty years of experience in social work and her demonstrated ability to meet with Portland's madams and persuade them to assist her in her work.

Women Unite to Save Womankind

The Oregon Daily Journal, April 16, 1905

Gentler Visitors to the Exposition Will Be Amply Protected.
Will Be Received in the Arms of Friends
Travelers' Aid Association Discusses Best Methods of Preventing Crime During Fair.

"This is a work that will succeed because it spells sisterhood!"

Dr. Stephen S. Wise so declared last evening at the meeting of the Travelers' Aid association held in the Unitarian church at Seventh and Yamhill streets. A large number of women gathered there to discuss the best methods of protecting girls who will come to Portland seeking employment during the fair....

His remarks were preceded by a statement of Mrs. Honeyman, president, in which she made clear the fact that hundreds of girls are coming to Portland to obtain situations, and that not all of them can be given employment.

"There is a frightful time ahead of us," said she, "unless we are prepared. We are promised help from all parts of the United States. We are to meet the boats, as well as the railroad trains, and we should have representatives uniformed to receive the girls who come here looking for work....

Mrs. Lola G. Baldwin spoke at length on her experiences here and elsewhere in work similar to that of the Aid association....

"We do not expect to eradicate the social evil in Portland," said the speaker, "but we do expect to improve it."

Mrs. Baldwin condemned the fake employment advertisements in newspapers, relating the incident of one man who insulted his stenographer after she had been in the office a few hours. This man's name, she said, was on the list, and he is under the watchful eye of the association. She reviewed her experiences in the north end, saying that that district is not wholly bad, as she had learned of several lodging houses that tried to carry on a straight business. She added that it was the purpose of the association to classify and index the lodging houses of Portland, designating them decent and indecent. The massage parlors and chiropodist establishments are also to be investigated, the speaker said, and put on the list....

The fake employment ads she mentions were apparently rampant at World's Fairs, scams by local brothels and ill-intentioned men looking to lure thousands of young women—many more than there were jobs for—who would then find themselves without work or enough money to return home and turning to a life of prostitution. While Baldwin prepared to care for and protect the young women when they arrived, she also attempted to counteract the ads in the hope of dissuading so many young women from coming at all.

Issues a Warning: Women Should Not Come to Seek Work: No Field for the Unskilled
The Sunday Oregonian, March 12, 1905

Portland Y. W. C. A. Fears That Many Young Women Will Come to the Fair Hoping to Secure Employment.

What shall be done to prevent the ills resulting from unemployed women hurrying to Portland, because it is Exposition year, in the hope of finding employment here?

That was the central thought underlying the meeting last night at the rooms of the Young Women's Christian Association, of the Portland Travelers' Aid Association and the various committees which are now being organized for the preventive work reported that 10,000 leaflets, 1000 placards and 5000 folders are being prepared to be scattered broadcast over the country. This literature is intended to reach unskilled young women workers who may think that all sorts of positions may be had here during the period of the Exposition, for the mere asking, and it is planned to send leaflets of advice to newspapers and magazines in the hope that such warnings may be published.

"We are all anxious that the right kind of visitors should come to this city and see the Lewis and Clark Exposition," said Mrs. Walter J. Honeyman, who presided, "but we may expect young women here who are not skilled at any particular trade or occupation, and they will land here expecting to get employment. In other words, they will be stranded. Who is going to take care of them, or furnish them with money to send them home?..."

Another woman remarked that she had lived in two different cities where expositions had been held, and that in each case tents and food along lines of private benevolence had to be provided.

"I heard of a case from Jefferson street depot," said Mrs. Tate. "A woman friend of mine was taking a girl she had just engaged to her home at Oswego, and left the girl at the depot for a few minutes while she made a purchase. In the interval a strange man approached the girl and asked her to go with him. She refused, and he offered to treat her and to give her theater tickets. She again refused, and he went away. When her employer returned the girl related what had taken place, and asked if she had treated the man right, and if she should have gone with him when he was so kind." It was decided that measures should be taken very soon, to work along preventive lines in meeting girls and women arriving at depots and ferries.

Lola Baldwin also addressed the issue of prostitution prior to, during, and after Portland's Lewis and Clark Centennial Exposition, as detailed in the following essay excerpt about her, coauthored by my grandmother.

Lola G. Baldwin

By Elizabeth S. Moorad and Wilma Crounse

With Her Own Wings, 1948

She visited known houses of prostitution, leaving her card and asking them to report to her any girls whom the thought she might help, warning them to take in no minor girl or to look out for prosecution. The results of this unusual procedure were surprising. Many times Mrs. Baldwin was quietly called to disreputable houses to take out girls who the management realized were too young and inexperienced for such a life. Of course, all these people were not cooperative, but they feared Mrs. Baldwin, and admired and respected her as well, knowing that she would never betray a confidence....

On one occasion she was called to an hotel where she met a man known to her to be powerful in the underworld. After some casual conversation she demanded to know why she had been called there. He said: "You are making too much trouble, and they say you will have to quit. How much do you want?" She replied: "I am on a salary and I don't need money. I am not going to quit." The man laughed and said: "I told them it wouldn't do any good, that they couldn't do a thing with *you*."

Another time a man came to her office in the evening, when she was alone, and offered her five hundred dollars to drop her efforts to convict a man accused of a crime. When she refused the money, he pulled a revolver from his pocket and threatened her. She faced him without flinching and said: "Go ahead and shoot." The man hesitated, lowered the gun and left the room, and the accused man was convicted and sent to prison.

Wilma Crounse, left, with Elizabeth Moorad. (Courtesy author's family archives.)

During the fair the House of the Good Shepherd became available for delinquent girls. A 1905 organizational meeting on the topic of establishing a juvenile court was not only successful, but organizers were also able to secure the respected Arthur L. Frazer as juvenile court judge. Also during the fair, Lola Baldwin and Millie Reid Trumbull advocated for the need to include girls as well as boys in the court's purview. When the court opened in June, Judge Frazer appointed Trumbull and Baldwin as head of the probation department and unpaid probation officer, respectively.

With all this work for Portland's public safety, it may not come as a surprise that Lola Baldwin was headed toward being named a police officer, but that was still a few years away. Portland's Lewis and Clark Centennial closed on October 15, 1905, and the city rejoiced at the wonder of it all. The fair was closed, but Lola Baldwin and others were still working to keep the Travelers Aid Society going.

Businessmen were proud that the project had turned a profit. But even before the fair ended, Travelers Aid Superintendent Lola G. Baldwin had discovered there were still women and girls in difficult circumstances. The problems dealt with during the four-and-a-half-month-long fair still existed—and would continue beyond the foreseeable future. Young women employed by the fair were afterward out of work with no means of returning home nor the qualifications for other work. Many who hoped to find respectable work in Portland were forced to take less honorable jobs after the fair ended.

While the fair was in town, notable cooperation between organizations, institutions, and individuals had demonstrated the will to assist with the efforts of the Travelers Aid Society. And when it ended, individuals and some city leaders voiced a desire to continue such assistance for young women and girls. However, with the end of the fair, two circumstances collided. On the one hand, many if not most of Portland's charitable organizations and religious communities assumed that their financial assistance would end when the Lewis and Clark Centennial Exposition was over. On the other hand, there existed a desire to carry on—both by the women involved with the work and by police leaders, who acknowledged the incredible preventive and protective work Lola and her aides had done—or at the least to raise enough money to continue the

Lola Baldwin at her desk. (Oregon Historical Society, #bb014193.)

work through the end of 1905. To their chagrin, organizations that had worked so willingly in conjunction with the YWCA during the fair were unwilling to continue afterward. That cooperative mood so evident during the fair largely evaporated, leaving a financial crisis.

For Travelers' Aid: Association Discusses Means of Continuance: What the Reports Show
The Morning Oregonian, October 20, 1905

At Least an Income of One Hundred Dollars a Month Is Needed for Keeping Up the Work So Well Begun.

Whether or not to continue the work of the Travelers' Aid Association or let it drop at the end of this month was a question seriously discussed at a called committee meeting of the organization yesterday afternoon in the Y. W. C. A. rooms, Sixth and Oak streets. The Travelers' Aid work was originally taken up for the Exposition period, but the necessity of continuous protective work in the interests of women and girls has so impressed itself upon the minds of those who have been immediately associated with the labors of the association that they hesitate to abandon a medium of accomplishing so much good without mature deliberation or making reasonable effort to obtain funds to carry it on through the year. It is estimated it will take about $100 a month to continue the work, but just where this amount is to come from has not yet been decided, for the committee members could come to no solution of the difficult problem and referred the matter to a committee composed of representatives from each of the various organizations making up the Travelers' Aid. It was shown by the superintendent's report that over 1500 women and girls had been assisted in various ways at the office of the association the past Summer, positions obtained for 60 girls, and that the publications sent out, in the form of cards of warning, identification cards, etc., has reached as far as Shanghai, China, a woman from there having applied for assistance and being helped through the local officers. The committee to be appointed will take up the question of just how to continue the work, and if it is deemed advisable it is likely that subscriptions will be asked.

Work of Exposition Board.

The work of the Exposition period has been very satisfactory and the association will come out about even on the financial part of the work up to the end of October. The treasurer, Mrs. C. R. Templeton, stated that while much had been sent from the East, the citizens of Portland and many organizations and lodges had materially assisted in the work....

Mrs. Lola Baldwin, superintendent of the local work, read a complete report of the October work, including a general review of the entire Summer's labors. She laid especial stress upon the number of children, especially little girls, who were permitted to travel alone, citing cases where those of very immature years came from far distant states to Portland and other Oregon points. Many of these were taken in charge by the Travelers' Aid, as relatives failed to meet them on arrival here and the children were practically lost. Individual cases of rescue and protective work were given, the inestimable service of the Travelers' Aid being shown in every instance. Girls who had disappeared were located by the superintendent and her aids and returned to their homes, and there were a number of weddings brought about through their influence. Men were prosecuted in the local courts for various offenses, in many cases not only the girl in question being protected, but the lesson taught the wrongdoers proving a protection to other girls.

Appreciate Travelers' Aid.

The Judge of the Police Court, Chief of Police and his officers have come to have a very high regard for the class of work accomplished by this association, for its workers are known to be women of determination and right instincts. The officers state that the Travelers' Aid has had a restraining influence upon procurers and other men of evil classes, and that their operations have not been so successful nor so open as they would have been had not the association workers been ever present at the railroads and wharves to meet incoming trains and boats.... ❧

Beyond the financial crisis, there was also a time crunch, as Lola Baldwin had some weeks earlier come up with the idea to do a nine-week cross-country tour to learn more about public safety tactics, particularly in relation to women and children, in other cities. She'd scheduled it for a mere two weeks after the close of the fair, thinking that would provide her plenty of time to plan and pack. Unfortunately, timing was proving to be inconvenient amid the budget meetings.

Baldwin departed for the East in early November 1905. Sadly for the TAS, it turned out that Lola's nine weeks away from Portland only exacerbated the issues. Whereas she had left town hoping that she had managed the situation, on her return she discovered the exact opposite to be true.

Baldwin covered thousands of miles during the ensuing nine weeks, covering her own expenses. This, she hoped, would allay concerns that the budget meetings were related to her travel. She fully understood that she must pay her own way or else it was quite likely that charges of graft would become an issue. Her first stop was in New York at her hometown of Rochester, where she visited with her mother and sister (whom it appears she had not seen since 1891). The city had witnessed a fair amount of wrongdoing in the police department over the past several years, and it would have taken very little to stir up public suspicions once again. But dating back to pre–Civil War days, Rochester had become a progressive community, and it was reasonable for Baldwin to wonder how such a city dealt with its young women and girls. She longed for time with friends and relatives, but she did not linger in visits. She also visited a telephone supply company that employed many girls among its four thousand employees.

She then traveled to New York City, where she spent a great deal of time visiting the national Travelers Aid headquarters and the Florence Crittenton mission on Bleecker Street, the Doyers Street mission located in the former Chinese Theater, then on to Chinatown, the Thanksgiving bread lines at the Bowery Mission, and New York City's settlement work, where playground and playrooms were being built to help get children off the street.

Baldwin also visited Washington, D.C., and Alexandria, Virginia. Discreetly, she did not stop in Burlington, Vermont, where her husband's parents lived. She may have been justified in doing so since the town's economy was in serious trouble and little money was available to help women and girls. Unfortunately, as it turned out she missed her last chance to see her husband's parents. A year later LeGrand received a mournful letter dated March 7, 1907, in which his father wrote, "It is with a sorrowing heart that I open these lines because a dear Mother has left us never to return...." Rhoda Caroline (Ray) Baldwin, LeGrand's mother, died on her fifty-ninth wedding anniversary. His father was inconsolable as he wondered, "Oh! How can I give her up, we have traveled together through so many years...." These words may have come to Lola's mind again thirty-four years later when her devoted husband, LeGrand, passed away in 1941.

Of note was Baldwin's visit to the Larkin soap company in Buffalo, New York, which employed seven hundred office girls. She was impressed that the company paid for its own YWCA secretary who catered to the needs of the working girls. Baldwin wrote letters home during her trip, each one reflecting her increased drive to continue the work to the best of her ability. It was not just about the young women in Portland; this was a national issue, and Portland could help advance the movement to protect girls and women across the country. Interestingly, Baldwin did not appear to know about the similar work that Sergeant Marie Connolly Owens was doing in Chicago, and she did not stop there on her cross-country educational tour.

Lola returned in the first week of January 1906, to more meetings about the future of the Travelers Aid Society and her public safety work in Portland. Although she received an anonymous donation of $500, the decision was made to dissolve the Travelers Aid Society in Portland and absorb it into the YWCA. The donor was later revealed to be James W. Cook, a salmon packer and vice property owner whose daughters were both members of Portland's Women's Union. On paper the TAS continued as it had during the Lewis and Clark Centennial Exposition—but minus the funding that had previously been donated by Portland organizations. The YWCA by itself could not afford to grant the TAS a budget of the size it had enjoyed earlier. The budget for 1906 consisted of the $500 from James Cook plus whatever donations Baldwin could drum up.

The meager funds disappeared sooner than expected, though, due primarily to the unexpected and horrendous April 18, 1906, earthquake in San Francisco, which caused rampant fires, killed more than two thousand people, left twenty thousand living in army tents, and sent seventy-five thousand more in search of help in other cities. Within a week hundreds of refugees began arriving in Portland, mostly by train. The *Oregonian* reported on April 27, 1906: "Great numbers of those who are arriving here are in the most destitute circumstances. Most of them have clothing, but no underwear. Scores of them come with burnt feet and practically no shoes."

As such, and with the help of a few smaller donations and subscriptions, the scaled-back program limped along for another couple of years—its work considered especially helpful after the San Francisco earthquake. By the end of 1906, community donations were sporadic in nature, at best, even with the TAS/YWCA's inclusion in the *Oregonian*'s Santa Claus list of "Some Places Where Christmas Cheer Is Needed."

When the financial panic of 1907 hit the nation, Lola Baldwin's funding efforts hit another wall. The panic also threatened layoffs and joblessness and was highest in the low-wage sector, with the result that an increasing number of young women were unable to find respectable jobs. Cases in which the police were involved with out-of-work young women suddenly more than doubled. Even though Baldwin's resources were thin, many of these unemployed women continued to be referred to her, as had been the practice since the exposition.

Many city officials were offering high praise for Baldwin's work. They were impressed by her ability when rising to serious threats, not to mention by her successes in court and her crime prevention techniques. Local, state, and national attorneys had witnessed many cases involving "Baldwin's girls" pass through their courts, and they also appreciated her work. City policemen called her at all hours of the day or night to handle cases involving women. At the same time, 174 police male detectives were struggling to get their jobs back during a police scandal in Portland. Her work was not involved in the scandal, and her accomplishments in Portland before, during, and after the fair served to further her reputation. Still, signs of solid financial support in the future were difficult to imagine in mid-1907.

Portrait of Portland Mayor Henry Lane. (Harris & Ewing, photographer. *Sen. Harry Lane, three-quarter length portrait, seated, facing slightly left*. Photograph. Retrieved from the Library of Congress, <www.loc.gov/item/97504326/>.)

While she often supplemented her program's budget with her own funds, providing some money or supplies to women and girls when she could, Lola Baldwin needed the city's financial support in order to continue her work. After consulting with a number of city officials, she was advised on the wisdom of appealing to Mayor Henry Lane for help. Baldwin then solicited Dr. Lane to request a measure of monetary support for her Travelers Aid program:

Dear Mayor Lane,

For three years, I have worn a star like any other member of the police department. Yet, the city has never paid anything for the service despite the fact that we have handled police cases almost every day. In 1906 our office worked 230 "special (i.e., vice related) girls." Through the end of November 1907 we have already handled 322, with no end in sight....

The time has come when Portland, as a city, should acknowledge the work, as three years of everyday demonstration given free of charge ought to be a fair test. The program's benefit to the area's young women and girls is obvious. We are asking that some provision be made in the 1908 police budget whereby this protective work for girls be carried on.... We do not ask to handle the money. Place it where you will, but let it be used for girls needing protection.

We notice that there was $5,030 used this year for the dog pound, and an additional thousand is asked for 1908.... [I make a request] for half that sum for practical, positive protection for the growing girlhood of the city of Portland.... Will you...place $3,000 to be used for the girls of Portland?

Despite political machinations, eventually the City of Portland granted Baldwin the $3,000 budget to continue her Travelers Aid work under the auspices of the police department. On April 1, 1908, Baldwin passed the civil service exam and was sworn in as a female detective, her official title reading: superintendent of the Women's Protective Division. While Lola G. Baldwin had been doing public safety work for years by then, she was now officially a policewoman.

The budget initially included hiring three policewomen, which were unfortunately cut back to just Baldwin and a full-time clerk, Miss Lucy May Sargent. Sargent resigned in 1909 when she married, and her position was filled by college graduate Wilma Pearl Chandler (later Crounse)—my grandmother. Wilma was immediately awarded with the unofficial title of assistant superintendent by Mrs. Baldwin. As with Sergeant Marie Connolly Owens in Chicago, both Lola Baldwin and her assistant were well suited for their work.

Portrait of Lola Greene Baldwin, who became an officer in 1908. (Portland Police Historical Society.)

Alice Stebbins Wells

Like Marie Connolly Owens and Lola Greene Baldwin, Alice Stebbins Wells found her way to an important calling. She was thirty-seven years old when she and her family moved to Los Angeles, where she immediately became involved in the city's welfare and ultimately requested a position with the police. Wells received quite a bit more publicity about this appointment than Baldwin or Owens did, and in short order the country was talking about the policewoman in Los Angeles, fascinated by the idea. She was often misidentified as the first policewoman in the world. The national discussion of women on police forces had started, and Wells—wanting to keep it moving—began to travel the country to speak on the topic and encourage the hiring of more and more policewomen.

Because Alice Stebbins Wells was in the spotlight for her advocacy for policewomen so much, there are more original sources about her, including her biographical information, than about the other two early policewomen. An excellent biographical summary comes from John Steven McGroarty.

Portrait of Alice Stebbins Wells, whose appointment in Los Angeles was highly celebrated. (Courtesy Los Angeles Police Museum.)

California of the South

By John Steven McGroarty

Volume V, 1933

The life history of Alice Stebbins Wells is an interesting one. She has been the leader in many movements of importance to the human race and a pioneer in some, notably in the policewoman movement. The position she has occupied for the past twenty-four years, that of policewoman in Los Angeles, requires talents which she possesses to a high degree. She has a strict sense of justice, a keen intellect, is guided by high ethical standards, and above all else has a desire to be of real service to mankind. She seems to have an intuitive knowledge of human beings, and has a genuine interest in them irrespective of station, race or creed. In reviewing her life work she seems to have a real desire to help as many as possible and to bring them to a realization of their latent possibilities. She firmly believes there is a little spark of virtue in every human being only waiting to be strengthened. No situation can daunt her courageous soul.

Alice Bessie Stebbins was born on June 13, 1873 in Manhattan, Kansas. A daughter of Homer Pease and Sarah (Kinney) Stebbins, both of whom were descendants of notable New England families and early graduates of Oberlin College, Oberlin, Ohio, where Mrs. Sarah Stebbins' father, Dean Daniel Kinney, was known for fifty years to all Oberlin students. Homer P. Stebbins taught Latin in the Oberlin schools, and later established and edited the first newspaper in Hiawatha, Kansas, a file of which is in the state capitol at Topeka.

Alice Stebbins was educated at Atchison, Kansas, graduating from the high school there. After leaving school she devoted several years to a business career in the Middle West, New York, and New England. About 1900 she became pastor's assistant for Dr. Newell Dwight Hillis in Plymouth Church, Brooklyn, made famous by Henry Ward Beecher, and following that she spent two years at the Hartford, Connecticut, Theological Seminary, specializing in Old Testament history with the intention of giving lectures on "The Message of the Prophets for Today." While attending the seminary she spent two vacations filling summer pulpits in Congregational Home Missionary churches in Maine, thereby becoming the first woman preacher in that state. She then gave her lecture course on the prophets with their civic message for our day at Chautauqua, Bible schools, and many churches throughout the East and Middle West, including Oklahoma.

She accepted a pastorate for a short time near Perry, Oklahoma. While in that state she married Frank Wells, a member of a pioneer Wisconsin family, whose eventual ill health necessitated her return to the professional field. Mr. and Mrs. Wells have three children: Ramona, who married Carl Horack, of Berkeley, California; Raymond Stebbins, who married Vera VanValer; and Gardner Stebbins, who married Carmen Modie. Both sons live in Los Angeles.

In May, 1910, having moved to Los Angeles, Mrs. Wells conceived the idea and undertook the work of securing the enactment of legislation creating the office of policewoman in this city. This undertaking was successfully concluded on August 13... of that year, and on this date she took the office, thus becoming the first regular policewoman in the United States and, so far as is known, the world.

This was such an innovation and a widening of the field for women, as well as helpful in character building for women and children, that interest was immediately aroused and in response to many appeals she lectured in scores of cities in the United States and Canada. Foreign countries were also deeply impressed with the movement and inquiries flooded her office. As the result of this agitation Mrs. Wells was able, in May, 1915, to call a conference for the purpose of organizing an international association of policewomen in Baltimore, Maryland, coincident with the National Conference of Charities and Corrections, now known as the National Conference of Social Work. She was elected president and served for five years. The movement had grown so rapidly that she was enabled to invite policewomen from fourteen states to this organizing convention. At the conference less than one year later the association membership represented twenty-two states, Canada and England. Their publications are interesting even to the layman, especially Mrs. Wells' first presidential address which was published in the annual conference proceedings, and Publication No. 1, which was printed and distributed the following year by the new policewomen's association.

In this she fixed the status of the word policewoman originally chosen by her as a distinct term pertaining only to regularly appointed city officers. Because of the novelty every woman given police power for any reason whatever was being called a policewoman; an erroneous appellation [that] often caused confusion and at times unjust criticism. She also urged training facilities in established centers because small cities were writing: "If we get the appropriation for a policewoman, can you recommend a trained woman officer who will come to us?" Mrs. Wells, in 1917, conducted the first university training class for policewomen at the first summer session held by the University of California in Los Angeles.

Mrs. Wells is a Republican and a Prohibitionist. She is the founder and the extension director of the Pan-Pacific Association for Mutual Understanding. She organized this association in 1924 and it has held interesting travel dinners featuring Pacific Coast counties ever since. She is a member of the Friday Morning Club, which was among the signers of her petition to create the office of policewoman. During 1927–1928 she was organizing chairman and first president of the Women's Peace Officers Association of California, which during its first year enrolled membership extending from San Diego to Humboldt County, and published as a yearbook the first compilation of women peace officers of the state. (Policewomen, police matrons, deputy sheriffs and deputy constables.) Within the last twenty years more than two hundred fifty cities in the United States appointed policewomen, and the number in Los Angeles increased to thirty-two. Mrs. Wells has held her position continuously since her appointment in 1910. Her latest activity is that of curator of the Los Angeles Police Department, appointed by James E. Davis at her request in order that she might establish a museum within the police department. Here are being gathered photographs, clippings from newspapers, pamphlets, equipment, etc., dating from the earliest days of the department down to the present time.

Somewhere along the way, most likely when she lived in Brooklyn or later in Los Angeles, Alice Stebbins Wells was exposed to the teachings of the French sociologist, criminologist, and psychologist Gabriel Tarde. Tarde believed that three processes exist in human society: invention, imitation, and opposition. It was his belief that:

> Invention…is the source of all progress. However, only one percent of people can make creative associations in their minds.… Imitation…is more widespread in society. Most people are not inventive, but only copy what they see from other people.… Opposition takes place when two or more inventions come into conflict with each other, or when new and old ideas collide. Oppositions may be associated with social groups, like nations, regions, or social classes, or may remain inside the minds of individuals. The outcome of opposition is often an adaptation.

Alice Stebbins Wells in the uniform she made herself in 1912. (Courtesy Los Angeles Police Museum.)

Professor Tarde also emphasized the tendency of the criminal to return to the scene of the crime and to repeat it, which he saw as part of a wider process of repetition compulsion. To the extent that Alice recalled any of Tarde's teachings in her later years, she may have benefitted from his concepts when she entered the field of criminal justice.

Later publications also focused on Wells and her contributions, which became even clearer as the policewomen movement unfolded. A 1951 article by Lois Higgins—quoting Chloe Owings's 1925 book, *Women Police: A Study of the Development and Status of the Women Police Movement*—explores the origins of the policewomen movement and sums up Wells's place in the public eye quite well, particularly in this excerpt:

Historical Background of Policewomen's Service
By Lois Higgins
Journal of Criminal Law and Criminology, 1951

Chloe Owings describes the reaction on the part of the press following the appointment of Alice Wells to the Los Angeles Police Department:

> The appointment of Mrs. Wells attracted wide newspaper comment because of the fact that she was an educated woman, a social worker, and had deliberately sought and secured the opportunity to work in a police department. Naturally, many journalists presented the situation in a half-comic manner and pictured the woman police officer in caricature as a bony, muscular, masculine person, grasping a revolver, dressed in anything but feminine apparel, hair drawn tightly into a hard little knot at the back of the head, huge unbecoming spectacles, small stiff round disfiguring hat, the whole presenting the idea in a most repellant and unlovely guise. This conception, however, was not universally held, and many groups of earnest women, searching for a solution of social problems greeted the idea of women police with favor, and Mrs. Wells was soon overwhelmed with requests for lectures and advice.

...In its efforts to extend the movement for women police service, the Women's Christian Temperance Union, through its president, Mrs. Sara Dow, in 1911, arranged a most extensive speaking schedule. In communicating with Chloe Owings, Mrs. Wells reported that this schedule was carried out to the exact letter. In thirty days, there were lectures in thirty-one cities.

The extension of the movement for women police, and the efforts made in its behalf were bringing results. These results could be seen in the report of the International Association of Policewomen which stated that in 1912, 1913, and 1914, seventy-three cities in the United States and Canada invited Mrs. Wells to one hundred thirty-six audiences. ❧

Various newspapers across the country printed updates on Wells and her training sessions and public speaking:

Ottawa Citizen (Ottawa, Canada), January 17, 1913: "Mrs. Wells is no academic speaker and speaks from a fund of knowledge acquired through actual experience and she is so earnest and of such a sweet and attractive personality as she presents her message concerning several grave problems and why there should be policewomen that sooner or later the civilized world must answer." ❧

Chicago Daily Tribune (Chicago, Illinois), January 22, 1913: "Resolutions were adopted by the Woman's City Club yesterday calling for the appointment of policewomen in Chicago. Mrs. Alice Stebbins Wells has just told the meeting of her work as policewoman in the police department of Los Angeles. Mrs. Wells urged the Chicago department to appoint women for patrol duty, for censors of public amusements and advisers of women." ❧

Lexington Herald (Lexington, Kentucky), circa 1913: "Womanly and winning, the first policewoman, Mrs. Wells, of Los Angeles, in her appearance in Lexington's afternoon at the courthouse under the auspices of the Civic League, the Moral Improvement League, the Advisory Board of the Juvenile Court and the Associate Charities, more than justified the commendatory things that have been said and written of her work." ❧

Washington Herald (Washington, D.C.), circa 1913: "Mrs. Alice Stebbins Wells gave an address last night on 'The Need of Policewomen and Their Work' in the Unitarian Church. Dr. U. G. B. Pierie, pastor and Chaplain of the Senate, introduced Commissioner Rudolph as chairman of the evening. The necessity of women police officers was explained. It behooves every municipality to provide women officials who can render help in many ways when man would be powerless. The policewoman's work is largely preventive. Mrs. Wells is small, and we who heard her talk in a low sweet voice would be apt to hazard a guess that she was a college professor or a litterateur." ❧

Letters of appreciation poured in for Wells too:

University of Pittsburgh, January 13, 1913: *I wish to express my appreciation of the address you delivered last night. It was most able, forceful, effective and convincing. The audience was delighted and instructed. The subjects you presented are fundamental to social well-being and you presented them in such a way as at once to disarm criticism and compel attention. The address cannot fail to bring about good results in Pittsburgh.*

Very sincerely,
B. McCormack, Chancellor.

Toronto, January 14, 1913: *Not in many years of social work and interest in social problems have I heard an address so comprehensive, so intelligent and so full of 1913 common sense as that to which we listened last evening. There is in this day no lack of speakers who criticize, but there is a dearth of speakers who are able to suggest as you did the preventive and educational measures which are practical. I am sure that your visit will prove of much benefit to our city.*

Faithfully yours,
A. McCarthy, Controller.

Beyond her public speaking, Wells also published many articles to help dispel myths about policewomen, clarify their roles and value, and inspire greater involvement among women. This 1913 article in *The American City* is representative of her ongoing message.

Women on the Police Force
By Mrs. Alice Stebbens [*sic*] Wells
The American City, April 1913

The arrival of the Woman Police Officer is a striking commentary upon the changed conditions of our day.

During the last half century the world has been frequently reminded that women could not be police officers and could not be soldiers. The police officer has arrived as a perfectly normal being and to fit a logical need.

The battles of the future will be intellectual and moral battles, and a vast army of women have been studying and working to prepare themselves as no body of soldiers has ever done before to help wage victorious warfare against the forces that would destroy the race.

Out of the many which might be named, two generally inclusive reasons for the woman police officer center our attention.

1st.—The police department is the great peace army. Its province is to keep the peace, to prevent crime through maintaining law and order.

During the last 25 years an active spirit of prevention has manifested itself in every line of human activity. A spirit based, no doubt, upon two deepest promptings—the quickening sense of brotherhood, of mutual responsibility, and the very self-preservation of the race under our increasing social complications. The woman officer has an emphasis upon the prevention spirit of police work.

2d.—To-day men, women and children face together industrial vicissitudes and socially commingle. Therefore, it now requires the best that both men and women can give, in the police department as elsewhere, to adequately meet the needs and properly handle men, women and children. Naturally, then, the woman's work concerns itself mostly with women and children.

There was no store for policewoman uniforms at the time, so they made their own. The regular uniform was dark blue, while the uniform for summer was lighter weight and green. (Courtesy Los Angeles Police Museum.)

I was appointed as a regular police officer in Los Angeles two years ago last September, a city ordinance creating the position having been passed in the regular way. In due time the civil service examination was called—the first of its kind—and, having passed it, the position became an integral part of the police work of our city. Since, we have added two more women, and other cities have done likewise.

Coming naturally under the domain of the woman officer are the places of amusement where the young gather—dance halls, skating rinks, picture shows, penny arcades, amusement parks, etc. Whenever it is necessary to make an arrest, the woman officer can make it, and carry the case through the court just as her brother officer would. I made 13 the first year, and had no serious difficulty. The proprietors are property owners, have interests at stake, and there would be no gain by resisting or refusing to appear upon summons.

I have office hours, and women come for help and advice for which they would not go to the regular police department. ❧

Alice Wells's recruiting effort became her most important contribution to the national—and international—emergence of policewomen. While touring the country and extolling the need for more policewomen, her speeches encouraged many women to join simply by describing her work. She was also featured in a documentary film titled *The Policewoman* in 1914.

It was not always positive, as some people protested the idea of women on police forces, but still, the movement had begun. By 1916 more than twenty-five cities in America and abroad had begun to hire policewomen, and in some places, women were even filling leadership roles. Dolly Spencer was one of the first, appointed chief of police in Milford, Ohio, in 1914, but promptly replaced by a man when a new mayor was elected. In 1915 Wells launched the International Policewomen's Association, which provided publications and conferences for policewomen. As the *Encyclopedia of Women in the American West* puts it, "This group allowed women to play a viable role in the continual advancement of their cause, enlightening the force and the position that women were playing in the development of departments across the nation." The association (later called the International Association for Women Police, or IAWP) is still an immense support to policewomen today, as will be seen throughout this book.

There's no question that these three women paved the way for future policewomen. Sergeant Marie Connolly Owens laid the groundwork with her appointment in 1891 in Chicago. She spent thirty-two years in the police force, and Chicago hired dozens more policewomen during her tenure. Superintendent Lola Greene Baldwin, unaware of Owens's work in the Midwest, fought for the Portland Police Department in Oregon to add her public safety program to the department's budget, finally receiving officer status in 1908. She retired in 1922 at the age of sixty-two and continued to volunteer her time and energy to social work for another thirty-five years. And Patrolwoman Alice Stebbins Wells brought the idea of policewomen to the national conversation, inspiring dozens of cities to hire from 1910 on, starting training programs, founding the International Policewomen's Association, and serving as the first president of the Women's Peace Officers Association of California. She transitioned to historian for the Los Angeles Police Department in 1934 and retired six years later. During these women's careers, through the 1910s and 1920s in America, the landscape of police departments—and women's lives in general—would change drastically.

Chapter 2
The Blooming of a New Age

The growth of the policewoman movement began after three women—Sergeant Marie Connolly Owens, Superintendent Lola Greene Baldwin, and Patrolwoman Alice Stebbins Wells—demonstrated the value of women in police-oriented work. Over time their unique abilities began to be appreciated, and other women sought to join the trend. This chapter recalls the successors of the earliest pioneers, primarily through original sources from that time frame. This new wave began in the early 1910s, when policewomen began to hold conferences; grew during World War I, when many of the country's men were deployed; and peaked around 1925, when Chloe Owings published her book *Women Police.*

The regions that saw the most growth included several cities in California and up the West Coast as well as Denver a little to the east; Chicago, Detroit, Indianapolis, and St. Louis in the Midwest; and of course New York. But the whole country was talking about women on police forces, and the advances made in these cities were a repeat topic in national publications like *The Survey* and *The American City*. The discussion of women taking on positions of authority in the early 1900s did not go without opposition, of course, which was also part of the national discussion at the time.

Western Women as Police Officers

The Survey, December 21, 1912

Every one knows that in the United States and other western countries the steady progress of women toward active citizenship and public service is gradually emerging from a nebulous into a more and more clearly defined state. Because the process is so even and widespread it is intangible, and we eagerly dissect all substantial indications of its growth. This is one reason why there has been considerable interest in the first conference of women police officers, held recently in Portland, Ore. The meeting drew attendance only from the Pacific Coast, but thus served the better to point out in what part of the country women police officers are taken for granted. At the close of three days' discussion it was decided to effect a permanent organization at Seattle at the time of the next National Conference of Charities and Correction.

Cities were variously represented: San Francisco by the travelers' aid secretary of the Y. W. C. A. who, with four assistants, comes in contact with 10,000 women and girls every year; Sacramento by a woman in the pay of the Southern Pacific Railroad and the Y. W. C. A., who works both in the station and out; Oakland by two representatives of its vice commission and the general secretary of the Y. W. C. A.; Seattle by both regularly appointed women members of its police force and a special police officer who works under the pay and auspices of the Y. W. C. A.; Spokane, North Yakima, Tacoma and other cities on the northwest coast by protective officers regularly appointed to the police force....

The view was expressed at the conference that a new movement for women protective officers in a community ought to be started under the auspices of a women's society. This would enable its possibilities and point of view to become well established before the work was brought into intimate relation with the police force. The change in the system may then usually be effected by an ordinance, although Portland thought it better to incorporate the reform into the city charter.

When the question of cost was brought up, figures were given to show that the *per capita* price of police protection last year had been $3.50 in New York, $2.43 in St. Louis, $2.46 in Philadelphia, and $2.13 in Chicago, whereas in Portland the cost had been $1.09.

Only through the appointment of women officers, declared the chief of police of Portland, can the problem of city vice be solved. He said if he put fifty men on burglary cases they would come back better and wiser; but if the same fifty were assigned to cases involving sexual immorality, the chances were that "in thirty days half of them would have fallen for the paint and powder and beguiling ways of the women who prey on man's weakness."

Three main conclusions seemed to rise naturally from the discussion. First, women will work harder than men to protect and save and will think less of punishment in dealing with those who are destroying themselves and others through vice. Second, women will do better work than men in cleaning up the vice conditions in a city. Third, women should be appointed on the pay roll of the city under some sort of supervision or co-operative work with volunteers of their own sex. It was declared that every city should have at least one [female] protective officer for every twenty-five policemen.

Eastward Trend of the Movement

Not in the extreme West alone are women police officers to be found, however. A year ago the movement reached Minneapolis, where as yet only one has been appointed. A month ago George Creel, Commissioner of Police of Denver, appointed a member of the detective bureau, Josephine Roche, who will be intrusted with the execution of the new dance hall ordinance and will aid in the fight against the social evil. Miss Roche was last year connected with the Vocational Guidance Survey of New York. Still more significant of the growth of the movement, however, is the fact there are three police women in Baltimore, and one woman detective in New York. A Maryland law of 1912 provided for five, calling them "matrons to the police force" to distinguish them from "station-house matrons."

Mary S. Harvey, for ten years connected with the Federated Charities, was the first to be appointed. Two months later Elizabeth Faber, a Swiss who speaks fluently English, French, German and Italian, and Margaret Eagleton, also connected with the Federated Charities, were named. Their work is varied. Minors of both sexes are looked after; moving picture parlors are watched; balls and dancing classes are supervised; prostitutes who are reported as entering a house of ill fame for the first time are visited. Any preventive or aggressive work that a woman can do seems to come what may be called police-woman's work.

The Philadelphia director of public safety, after listening to the arguments of Alice Stebbins Wells, of the Los Angeles police force, announced that he would request at once the appropriations necessary to employ women detectives. Mrs. Wells is visiting various parts of the country to widen her acquaintance with police methods and conditions elsewhere, and incidentally she is securing publicity for arguments for putting women in uniforms. ❧

That "eastward trend of the movement" was made evident by many articles about specific cities adding women to their police departments. Chicago was adding to its force, although the following article, oddly, does not mention that Owens had already been part of the force for some time. It does, however, note the controversy over whether the so-called weaker sex could do police work effectively.

Policewomen in Chicago

The Literary Digest, August 23, 1913

Chicago's latest novelty in the establishment of a squad of policewomen on the regular force is not an innovation so real as apparent, in the view of some editorial observers, among them *The Wisconsin State Journal* (Madison), which calls attention to the fact that "within the last few months

Ten newly appointed policewomen, Chicago, Illinois. They are (left to right): Anna Loucks, Clara Olsen, Fannie Willsey, Margaret Wilson, L. C. Parks, Margaret Butler, Alice Clement, Emma F. Neukon, T. D. Meder (supervisor), and Gertrude Howe Britton (supervisor). (DN-0060955, *Chicago Daily News* negatives collection, Chicago History Museum; photo has been cropped.)

all over the country women have been appointed on the police force, even in States which do not have equal franchise.["] In this connection it is even remarked by some that Chicago's ten original policewomen "ought to be able to demonstrate very speedily the wisdom of the Illinois Legislature in giving women the vote," while others, noting that unquestionably there is special work cut out for the policewomen, offer in evidence, among their several qualifications, the experience of many European countries that the policewoman is "the best and most effective agent" in the fight against "the monster of modern society" known as "the white slaver." Of the ten Chicago women added to the staff of Chief of Police McWeeny by appointment of Mayor Harrison, we read in the press, eight are widows. Their ages run from twenty-five to fifty and their height from five feet two inches to five feet ten. Their weight ranges from 100 pounds to 170 pounds. The present appointments, we learn, are for a period of sixty days, after which the Civil Service Commission will hold regular examinations for the positions. The particular duty of the policewomen, it is generally forecasted, will be to see to the protection of women and children; altho, with the full authority of a policeman, they will have to be prepared to meet whatever exceptional duty chances on their beat. But this is just where the trouble comes in, according to the New York *World*, which questions the wisdom of Chicago's new move, altho it admits that:

> There is plenty of police work that women might do to advantage. As sanitary police, as special officers of the Health Department, they certainly would not prove more inefficient or careless than men. All the business of the police is not to deal with criminals and rowdies and violent persons of both sexes. But there is emergency work any policeman must be ready to do at a moment's notice. When Officer Blank, in natty blue jacket and skirt, with star on her breast, hears of a hold-up or murder in a low dive on the Levee in Chicago, what is she going to do? Will she seize the murderer red-handed, wrest his smoking pistol from him, and march him off to the corner, bruised and subdued, to wait for the wagon, while a mob clamors for his life? Until Chicago has settled this delicate question of a woman's physical disability for the rougher duties of the police, less progressive communities will probably prefer to wait and get along as best they can in the old-fashioned way.

In complete disagreement with such a stand is the Chicago *Daily News*, holding that Chicago's policewomen signalize the passing of the old notion that "any officer of the law must be a heavy-footed and more or less slow-witted male person armed with a formidable club and a revolver." We are reminded that New York and Chicago have some time since discovered the superiority as policemen of the "clean-limbed, alert, tall, and vigorous" type of a young man, and *The News* adds:

> But the appointment of women to the police force goes further and throws the emphasis upon sympathy and understanding instead of upon mere muscle. Tho the new appointees constitute a novelty, they will doubtless be able to discharge their duties effectively, for the conditions have long been preparing for just such a departure. The success of women as probation officers and in other positions of trust and responsibility has prepared the women themselves and also the community for women police officers. Chicago welcomes its new

> guardians and is well assured that they will prove their usefulness on bathing-beach and playground and in public dance halls and other places where the young, and especially young girls, are exposed to peculiar dangers.

Along this line the Charleston *News and Courier* points out as a defect of American police systems that they have not properly dealt with the white-slave traffic, which "grew to immense proportions before the police really knew what was going on," whereas in Europe policewomen have won a splendid record for themselves in this field of activity. The Police Commissioner of Scotland Yard, *The News and Courier* tells us, testified before the International Congress in London that in this crusade he believes the assistance of policewomen "to be essential to success," which leads the Charleston paper to suggest:

> If the woman policeman is really the best instrument which the law can find with which to combat the evil which probably costs American more than any other country on the globe, by all means let us have women policemen at once. We can go to school to Europe for learning of many sorts, and perhaps this is a matter in which we can profit from her experience. ❧

The white slavery that this and several other articles of the time mention refers to kidnapping women for sex work. The White-Slave Traffic Act of 1910, also known as the Mann Act, made transporting women for this purpose a felony, and many cities were attempting to enforce it strictly. As policewomen were already focusing on public safety for women and children, many dealt with sexual slavery on some level.

The Police-Woman Is Marching On

The American City, November 1913

It was not so very long ago that the mere mention of the term "police-woman" could be depended upon to provoke a smile. There are those who still regard the idea as inherently humorous; have they not seen many faithful caricatures in magazines and newspapers of an Amazon crowned with the old-time helmet, clad in blue uniform with a liberal supply of brass buttons, and *always* brandishing a club?

Now that the police-woman dwells no longer in the realm of fancy, but has become a potent factor in the life of many of our cities, we find she bears little resemblance to her spurious portraits. She is usually quiet, often slight in build, filled with the seriousness of her work, and has no use for the big stick. She comes into a field that has long been waiting for her. Much of the work she takes up has not been done by men; it has simply been left undone because men were not fitted to do it.

Quite recently the city of Chicago added ten women to its police force. Mayor Harrison's plea for women police contains the following words:

"There are certain classes of police work that can be performed much better by patrol-women than by ordinary patrolmen.

"In the supervision and care of dance halls, bathing beaches, small parks and playgrounds, in the performance of duties connected with Juvenile Court and other kindred matters, greater care and appreciative attention to the morals and physical requirements of girls may be expected from police-women than from ordinary policemen, who necessarily become hardened to some extent by reason of the character of the services they are called upon daily to perform."

The Kansas City Board of Police Commissioners announce that the police-woman recently appointed by them is to be "the city's mother to the motherless." Her way lies through a section composed largely of disorderly resorts and all-night cafes. One of the commissioners referred to has said:

"We will consider the Police Department amply repaid if we save from wrong living a half-dozen girls, but we expect the police-women to do far more than that."

The police-woman has not been in office long, but in some cities she has already served long enough to prove her value. The work of such a woman as Josephine Roche, until lately a member of the police force in Denver, would refute any statement to the effect that police-women are not needed.

Mr. George Creel, in a recent number of the *Metropolitan*, has given a most interesting account of Miss Roche and her work in Denver...:

"From the start Miss Roche was an amazing sort of cop, for all her energies were devoted to avoiding all necessity for arrests. When she made the rounds of the amusement places she didn't say, 'Do so and so or I'll lock you up.' What she did was to talk long and quietly with every sullen, resentful man of the lot, citing instances of assault and seduction growing out of the nightly swarming of mere children about rink and show and hall, showing the stain of shame and tears on many a dime, and appealing to their sense of decency and love of family.

"Wholesale arrests would have only accentuated ugliness and perpetuated opposition. Miss Roche's policy turned every proprietor into an active supporter of the ordinance; and boys and girls under sixteen, unless accompanied by parents, are no longer seen in dance halls, skating rinks and moving picture shows of Denver."

Josephine Roche, a detective in Denver. (Harris & Ewing, photographer. *Josephine Roche.* Photograph. Retrieved from the Library of Congress, <www.loc.gov/item/2016880304/>.)

The further accounts Mr. Creel gives of Miss Roche's influence on the boys' "gangs" and her work for fallen women convince one that Miss Roche was not an ordinary police-woman, but they also strengthen one's belief in the existence in all cities of a big and vitally important work for women police.

It is less of a problem to get laws enacted than to get them enforced. Heretofore our cities have overlooked one of the best aids to the enforcement of all laws relating to women and children. Now they are slowly opening their eyes—such cities as Los Angeles, Chicago, Kansas City, Portland, Baltimore, San Antonio, Rochester and Tacoma—and by adding one or more women to their police force have become pioneers in a movement which we believe will continue to spread throughout the entire nation. ❧

Roche in 1940. (Harris & Ewing, photographer. *Miss Josephine Roche, Jan. 1940.* Photograph. Retrieved from the Library of Congress, <www.loc.gov/item/2016877012/>.)

Police Women's Efficiency in Danger

The Survey, May 2, 1914

Some of the most influential clubs and civic organizations of Chicago have protested vigorously against the action of Chief of Police Gleason in regard to the city's twenty policewomen. Under Second Deputy Superintendent Funkhouser, the civilian police official, they have proved effective in regulating public dance halls. Under Second Deputy Superintendent Schuettler, to whose command they have been transferred, they are assigned to regular police duty, scattered among various station houses, and can no longer be used for inspection of dance halls or other pieces of work requiring concerted action.

In making over 1,500 inspections of dance halls, in which they found many violations of law for which arrests might have been made, the women officers, being more intent upon prevention than punishment, determined to make no arrests at first, but to warn the managers and to win the girls who patronize the dances. This policy has proved successful in securing obedience to law and observance of propriety.

Such results in the dance halls made the second deputy's administration a shining mark for assaults from the underworld, just as his strict censorship of motion pictures has attracted opposition from those who made and promote films suggestive of evil. Such enemies of public safety and common decency are believed to have found aid and comfort at the hands of certain police officials and of others higher up.

It is feared that the fine *esprit de corps* of the new women police will suffer by being forced to conform to the varying standards of the stations to which they have been assigned.

The ostensible reason for taking them away from Major Funkhouser is that his use of their service transcends his function as the civilian deputy and belongs to the active force. But his squad of male officers is left under his command, apparently without fear of inconsistency, perhaps because under the surface it is not inconsistent with the purpose dictating the transfer of the women.

By 1914 the American policewomen movement was drawing attention from Europe as well, and the following publication in England made the case for English policewomen whose duties would be similar to those of Chicago's Alice Stebbins Wells and Denver's Josephine Roche.

Policewomen: Their Work in America

By Maud Darwin

The Nineteenth Century and After, June 1914

It is the great change in social custom which has made the institution of policewomen desirable.

A century ago teaching was almost the only profession open to educated women, while domestic service still absorbed by far the greater number of the uneducated. To-day all this has changed. A huge army of women and girls leave home daily to work in countless different shops and offices and factories. It is estimated that in London alone over half a million women under thirty-five earn their own living, and that two thirds of the girls between fifteen and twenty-five are employed either in commerce or in industry. The general public in a town is no longer composed almost entirely of men. Places of amusement, as well as factories, are crowded by young people of both sexes. Women are, in fact, no longer confined, either in their work or in their play, to their own homes or to those of other people. This increased publicity of their lives has made the establishment of the woman police officer an urgent necessity in our towns.

The institution of policewomen is not intended to displace that of policemen in any way. Their work is merely supplementary. The policewoman has the same authority as the policeman; she can arrest people; but it is not her business to drag drunkards to the police station, to trap a burglar, or to direct traffic. That is a man's work. The women's work is chiefly preventive in character. She must prevent people from breaking the law, rather than catch them after the offence. Her chief duty is to guard young girls and boys in all public places. As the love of outdoor life grows, parks and open spaces in towns have become increasingly frequented, whilst dancing-halls and skating-rinks, picture palaces and theatres are crowded every evening by young people in search of relaxation. In all these places she is much needed at the present day. From the experience of another country, we can learn what her exact duties should be. Conditions of life in the United States of America are slightly different from those in England—women there being probably rather less bound by traditional conventions; but there is so much similarity in the town life of both countries that these differences are not of any real importance.

* * *

It was in a school at Salt Lake City, Utah, early in 1913 that I chanced upon Mrs. Wells, the first American to conceive the idea of adding women to the police force, and the first woman to be so appointed. When I was told of her profession my imagination flew to the typical figure of a policeman in London, and I pictured her a strapping Amazon in uniform, bâton at waist, helmet on head, and on her feet the boots so familiar to us in the stage farce. When I encountered my first policewoman I was disillusioned. I found her not an Amazon but a slightly built, active woman a little over five feet in height. Her age was between thirty-five and forty. She had a pleasant firm voice and bright blue eyes which seemed to me to be more than usually observant. As one newspaper described her, she was "about as formidable as a kitten." She had come to Salt Lake City at the request of the civic authorities to tell them of her duties, as they were considering the question of appointing women to the police force there. Her work at Los Angeles in California had been so widely appreciated, and her superiors in office had received so many letters of inquiry regarding it from the authorities of

Women police receiving handgun training. (*Women Police Officers Inspecting and Practicing with Handguns.* [Between 1910 and 1920] Photograph. Retrieved from the Library of Congress, <www.loc.gov/item/95502501/>.)

other towns, that they decided to allow her six months' leave of absence, in order that she might travel and tell other municipal authorities about her work....

There are now three women police in Los Angeles and four women probation officers. The policemen there approved of the new appointments. One of them said to a reporter that it was the most sensible thing the police department had done. Others said that they should have been put on the force long ago. The chief of the Los Angeles police wrote:

> Through suffrage, recognition of policewomen in Los Angeles has been obtained and crime materially reduced. It is obvious that when women have no voice in municipal control, the employment of their services in the war against crime is improbable.

I have a copy of a testimonial from the Sheriff, who writes:

> It is a well-known fact that a young girl, no matter how depraved she may be, dislikes to unfold her tale of woe to a man. Therefore I believe that there should be a department of the police separate and distinct from the regular police to be presided over by a woman, who should have a sufficient number of assistants and whose duties it would be to take charge of matters wherein women and young girls are concerned.

The City Clerk of Los Angeles writes:

> There is no question that the field thus occupied is one long neglected in the interest of young women, and it would not be possible to persuade the inhabitants to abolish this new service and this work now; rather do we feel it is only begun, and it will be enlarged as the importance of the work grows upon our townspeople.

A probation officer writes:

> I believe that women in police work are as necessary as in probation work, and that women's and girls' problems in police departments should handle girls' cases in our Juvenile Courts. Common decency and delicacy should have made these things obvious long ago.

In Denver, Colorado, there has been a woman in the police force since 1912. I was told in 1913 by friends living in the town that she had revolutionised the treatment of the young offender. "The best man on the Denver police force happens to be a woman," said the chief of the police....

In her own words, she said:

> I do not believe that a woman is any more capable or conscientious than a man in the long run, but it is only natural that she should be able to do some things better than a man can, just as a man can do some things better than a woman. Women by nature are more interested in children. They understand them better, and therefore are better fitted to deal with the great child-problem of the day. That is why I believe women have come on the police force to stay. They are the ones to deal with juvenile delinquency. Besides this, we no longer believe in the old theory that law must be enforced by the club or the revolver. You cannot force people to do right. You cannot beat goodness into them. You have to show them why they should obey the law. Just because a woman is a woman and disassociated from the idea of force, she can frequently enforce the law with more ease than a man. The main thing is to be on the job constantly and let people know they are being watched.

It is impossible to say how many policewomen there are now in the towns of the United States. Six months ago there were thirty-eight, but I am constantly hearing of their appointment in new towns. In Pittsburg four have recently been added to the force.... They must be between thirty and fifty years of age. Their duties are to visit hotels and all other places of public resort frequented by girls and women. They are to attend magistrates' hearings and assist girls and women who are involved in charges. They are given broad powers of making arrests on suspicion. They are to wear badges marked "Pittsburg Auxiliary Police."

Every town makes its own regulations for the policewomen as they are appointed. In some a uniform is to be worn, in others there is no uniform. In one town a policewoman must be five feet eight inches tall, in others there is no qualification as to height.

For three or four years the women in Chicago had petitioned for policewomen again and again, but their request was always politely refused until they were enfranchised, when within three months ten women were put on the force. The result has been so satisfactory that in January this year the Superintendent of Police asked the City Council for sufficient funds to employ fifteen more women....

A Bill has just been introduced in the Assembly of New York State for the appointment of women police for New York City. The Bill requires the Police Commissioner to appoint twenty patrolwomen and as many more as he deems advisable. They must be citizens of the United States, of at least five feet eight inches in height, and between thirty and forty-five years of age. They are to receive the same salary as patrolmen. They may be ordered on duty at public parks, dance halls, places of amusement, or on patrol duty in the streets....

It is interesting to note that a year ago two policewomen were appointed in Toronto. They are "sworn-in constables" with full powers of arrest. They are paid two-thirds of the salary of policemen for the same amount of work. They were appointed at the request of the local council of women, who convinced the members of the Police Commission that there were branches of the work, especially with regard to prostitution, which could be more adequately dealt with by women constables. The problem of prostitution had hitherto hardly been touched by the police. Frequent observation showed that the women employees, when leaving the large shops and factories, were subject to annoyance from bad characters. This was also the case in the public parks and places of amusement. It is hoped that the establishment of these two women will help towards a better state of affairs.

A few years ago the very idea of policewomen was absurd. In the 'sixties Leech held them up to ridicule in *Punch*, in an amusing picture in which he represented them as small-waisted creatures, clad in policemen's jackets and helmets, with crinolines reaching to their knees. But the idea which still seems so absurd to many in England has not been deemed impracticable elsewhere. America is not the only country where policewomen have been appointed. They are to be found in most of the large cities of Germany, Holland, Denmark, Norway, Sweden, Austria and even Russia. Yet England is still without them! The time has now come, in my opinion, when the police department of every town in England should have in its employment one or more women to whom girls and women can come for help and advice, and whose duties would be analogous to those of the policewoman in other countries.

In America, the policewomen movement was picking up enough steam that various cities were not just requesting but *requiring* police departments to hire women. Some of this was a wartime call to action for more civil support from those who remained in the country while soldiers were fighting abroad or were recuperating as they returned home, as the following article briefly mentions.

Women of the New York police force. (*Police Women - Capt. Edyth Totten and women police reserve. New York City.* Photograph. Retrieved from the Library of Congress, <www.loc.gov/item/2006675559/>.)

Policewomen and Their Work

By Ellen A. O'Grady

The American City, Police Departments, January 1919

New York, N. Y.—The New York women police are divided into two forces, one a paid force and the other volunteer. The former has, at the present time, a membership of 18 and the latter a membership of 5,000.

The paid force consists of eight women who are regular members of the Police Department, have passed civil service examinations, and are entitled under the law to pension rights. They receive a salary of $1,350 per annum. The other ten were appointed under a special act of the State Legislature, for the duration of the war. Their salary is $1,200 per annum. They are all under the supervision of the Fifth Deputy Commissioner. The volunteer class are recruited from prominent social welfare workers. They are trained under the supervision of regularly assigned members of the Department.

Parade of New York policewomen. (Bain News Service, Publisher. *Policewomen, N.Y.* Photograph. Retrieved from the Library of Congress, <www.loc.gov/item/2014706979/>.)

The duties of these policewomen are to safeguard the morals of young women in the vicinity of cantonments and camps; to investigate crimes affecting women, such as compulsory prostitution, abortion cases and fortune-tellers. They also look after the wayward and missing girls, juvenile delinquents, and cases of improper guardianship. They secure employment for worthy girls and women, act the part of peacemakers in family difficulties, and, in fact, do general welfare work. They are assigned from Police Headquarters to various zones all over the five boros of Greater New York.

The volunteer organization is recruited from the women residents of the city, and they are organized into precinct units. Their duties are to discover irregular and unlawful conditions and to report them to the regular Police Department; to teach patriotism and civic duty and aid in the Americanization of the alien elements of the population; to detect and report cases of disloyalty and sedition; to relieve cases of distress and destitution, comfort the unfortunate; advise and direct the weak, foolish and idle; set an example of unselfish patriotic devotion; and look after boys and girls who may be prone to be delinquent, keeping bad company or pursuing such a course as would lead to crime. Women of ability and character are sought by precinct commanders as members, and the responsibility of choosing the right kind of women is placed on the police captains.

Drills in infantry tactics are frequently held at suitable places within the precinct in which the policewomen are enrolled, for the purpose of instilling discipline. Lectures on the subject of police and other civic duties are frequently given.

Motor and ambulance corps have been organized for duty in the event of a great emergency. This branch is at present rendering very useful service in making the lot of our wounded soldiers lighter by taking them out in automobiles on interesting sight-seeing tours. In precincts where benches, parks and other public resorts are located, the women are rendering very useful service in safeguarding the morals of young girls in their chance acquaintance with members of the opposite sex. ❧

By the early twenties, Indianapolis, Indiana, boasted the largest force of policewomen, seemingly to counter its reputation as the Port of Missing Women.

The Policewomen of Indianapolis and Their New Methods

The Literary Digest, April 23, 1921

Indianapolis has the largest department of policewomen in the world, and their success in handling crime has lately turned the steps of numerous public-safety officials to the Indiana city where they operate to see how they do it. There seems to be one outstanding difference between this "feministic" police organization and most others. Capt. Clara Burnside, supervisor of policewomen, and her twenty-three assistants, make a special point to avoid arrests. Jail sentences and a large record of convictions, the standard upon which the efficiency of most police organizations is based, are not considered important. They handle most offenders "in a little court of their own," we are told. William Herschell, writing in the Indianapolis *News*, gives some details of the work and organization of the unit:

> The Indianapolis department of policewomen, organized in June, 1918, with eleven members, now has a roster of twenty-three women with women in command. Washington has the

next largest separate department, with twenty-one members. Seattle has a force of seven women, and Detroit now has a department undergoing organization. New York, Chicago, and St. Louis have women attached to their "finest," but not as separate units.

The Indianapolis Board of Public Safety recently promoted Miss Clara Burnside, supervisor of policewomen, to the rank of captain, a recognition of service that has attracted national attention. Mary Egan has been named sergeant of the department.

The 1920 report of the department of policewomen showed conclusive proof of the great public value of the policewomen's department...:

Captain Clara Burnside of the Indianapolis police force. (Courtesy Lichtenberger History Room, Indianapolis Metropolitan Police Department.)

> We consider the department of policewomen one of the most effective and efficient arms of the police organization in Indianapolis. We have endeavored to place the department on a substantial footing and, under the direction of Miss Burnside, it has shown itself capable of great work. It is a credit to the city and we and we hope to see it enlarged to meet every need. The work of the department is not generally appreciated, and it will not be, because of the necessity for secret operation. The public never hears of hundreds of cases silently but effectively handled without arrests....

Miss Burnside, for years an efficient attaché of the juvenile court, had gained the confidence and respect of every man in the police department.... She constantly is on the job, striving to right some domestic ship that threatens to go on the rocks, or seeking, with the aid of her loyal force of policewomen, to make some erring girl take the better path.

One of Miss Burnside's greatest difficulties was that of obtaining the cooperation of all the law-enforcing agencies. Many of the men looked on the policewoman idea as just another fad, just another agency for the reckless squandering of the taxpayers' good money. That attitude has been reversed. Every unit of the police department, the courts, the social, the social betterment societies, and civic organizations, has voiced complete approval of the new system of handling the intimate affairs of women and girls who have made human mistakes.

The policewomen of Indianapolis do not wear uniforms. Instead they go clad as they would go to market or to the shops—just the real women "human-bein'ism" stamped on their souls. They are, in effect, detectives or "plain-clothes men." If they wore uniforms they could easily be detected by shoplifters and other violators of law. As it is they go into the stores, mingle with the crowds, and, because of their every-day appearance, are not detected at their work.

There is a tremendous interest in the work shown by all the members of the department. This is one of the essentials of its success. The women believe in their work and are thoroughly alive to its aims. The result is a hard-working, conscientious force of capable women embarking in a new field, but accomplishing every result predicted for the department. They are proud of the fact that they are members of the largest department of policewomen in the world. They command respect wherever they go, both from the standpoint of personality and from their high efficiency....

The department deals not alone with women. Many of those arrested and convicted by policewomen in 1920 were men, sixty-three having been charged with most serious offences. In nearly every instance these men received long sentences in penal institutions.

The policewomen were responsible for the apprehension of sixty-four shoplifters last year. This is by far the greatest number of shoplifters arrested in Indianapolis in one year, and it was due almost entirely to the effective work of the women on the floors of department stores in the holiday season. Of the number [apprehended] twelve were juveniles.... Of the sixty-four apprehended only eight were arrested. The remainder were brought to the office of Captain Burnside and there signed statements indicating that they had stolen articles and were released without court procedure. In nearly all of these cases the offenders were neither habitual criminals nor of bad reputation. They had succumbed to temptation. The effectiveness of this work is testified to by that only two of the women picked up by the police have repeated their offenses....

The annual report of the department says that "during the holiday season the number found shoplifting was much smaller than in 1919 and the articles taken were for the most part of small value." This writer comments:

This is a real testimony to the efficiency of the department, for in previous years the loss to merchants in the holiday seasons alone was estimated at several thousand dollars.... ❧

Informal portrait of Mrs. Agnes Walsh, a policewoman, loading a handgun in Chicago, Illinois. (DN-0071148, *Chicago Daily News* negatives collection, Chicago History Museum.)

Policewomen in Indianapolis had many of the same duties as policewomen in Chicago, Portland, Los Angeles, and so on, including protecting girls in parks and dance halls, assessing their home lives and need for employment, handling cases of missing persons, and monitoring the appropriateness of films shown in theaters, all with Burnside's emphasis on intervening rather than arresting whenever possible. The article closes with a call for more of the same: "The effectiveness of the work being done by Captain Burnside and her department is causing the Board of Public Safety to consider additions to the women's unit."

As Detroit, Michigan, built their force of policewomen, the director of the Women's Division, Virginia M. Murray, wrote of their plans to formalize divisions and respective duties within the force and laid forth boundaries on the type of women and girls they were prepared to aid.

Policewomen in Detroit

BY VIRGINIA M. MURRAY

The American City, Forward Steps in Municipal Affairs: Police Departments, September 1921

Detroit, Mich.—The profession of the policewoman is new and not thoroughly understood. Some of the earlier choices for the work were unfortunate, as the interpretation of the policewoman's function was that of the old police strong arm methods and along punitive rather than protective and preventive lines. The newer interpretation contemplates a much broader scope and a more effective service. For a successful working basis certain fundamental factors are recognized:

1. The need for trained personnel. The so-called delinquent girl, or the girl on the border line of delinquency, presents quite the most complex problem in the field of social service, and to deal with the various elements found in this type of girl requires intelligent and expert service.

2. The place of the policewoman in the community is a definite one. She should not usurp the function of other organizations, such as probation or parole officers, employment bureaus, or the private protective agency. Her largest service can be done by utilizing all these other agencies for the continued oversight of the girl who may have first come under the notice of the policewomen, but who needs constant and individual care over some definite period of time for the purpose of reestablishing her in society. The unit by which policewomen measure their success should not be the number of arrests made, but rather the number of arrests prevented.

The new Women's Division of the Detroit Police Department, just now in the process of organization, is based upon this understanding of function. For the purpose of administration, the Women's Division has four different departments:

1. Protective
2. Under-Cover
3. Patrol
4. Office

The women assigned to the Protective Department are in and about the commercialized amusement places, railway and interurban stations, or wherever young girls are likely to be in any considerable number. Their first duty is not to arrest these girls, but to try to discover if they are in any moral danger, and if so, plan to refer them to other organizations already existing, or to their parents, to give them any further oversight needed.

Under-Cover work is the securing of confidential information on various matters without the identity of the policewomen being known. Frequently the most valuable and most authentic facts are so obtained, upon which definite arrests may be made or other necessary action taken.

The Patrol Division is upon the streets for the discovery of law violations which involve women and girls.

The Office Department looks after investigations, interviews, and complaints, and decides what action should result from certain information thus obtained. Sometimes this involves mental and physical diagnosis and working out plans for constructive treatment. Too much emphasis cannot be laid upon the necessity of trained women for this work.

For the present the Detroit policewomen are confining their efforts to work with girls between the ages of 17 and 21 years and all women and girls who are first offenders, because the state provides no constructive treatment or care for the woman with fixed habits of misconduct. The policewomen are planning only to study this group who are known as "repeaters" for the purpose obtaining social, physical and mental data, in order to emphasize the need for state custodial care over a longer period of time.... ❧

The American City's profile on policewomen in St. Louis, Missouri, showed that the movement had spread to all areas of the country and that their work was well appreciated.

Effective Work of Policewomen

By John A. Brandenburger

The American City, Police Departments, March 1923

St. Louis, Mo.—The Policewomen's Bureau of the Police Department of St. Louis is making a splendid record. It was created in 1916, with a staff of four women. In 1918 eleven more were added and a woman supervisor was placed in charge. Several months later the Women's Bureau was placed under the jurisdiction of the Chief of Detectives. The investigations conducted by this Bureau cause the arrest of persons and the issuance of warrants charging them with various offenses, among which are the following: assault and battery, assisting in burglary, kidnapping, petit larceny, violating the

Mann white slave act, violating postal laws, abandoning wife and children, deserting the Army and the Navy and such minor offenses as begging, disturbing the peace, fortune telling, incorrigibility, etc.

The policewomen have investigated almost [every] kind of case in which the moral and physical welfare of young girls is involved. Their work includes the apprehension of fake doctors and fake specialists, the investigation of letters of inquiry from other cities, the patrolling of the congested downtown districts, particularly department stores and motion picture shows, protective and preventive work with young girls who flock into the city, the assisting and directing of travelers and other work in connection with the Travelers' Aid. The reports of all missing persons are forwarded to the Policewomen's Bureau, and to them is assigned the work of locating these persons. Intensive work is given to the investigation of missing and runaway girls, and special effort is directed to the arrest of persons who violate the law by contributing to the delinquency of these girls.

Two of the policewomen are assigned to assist in the work connected with the Venereal Clinic and the Mortality Squad. Policewomen assume various disguises and take various positions in order to accomplish results. Some thrilling stories result from their experiences....

A Mother of Disillusioned Girls in New York City

The Literary Digest, March 15, 1924

Runaways of all sorts turn naturally to the big cities, and that is one reason why Mrs. Mary Hamilton, assistant to Police Commissioner Enright of New York City, has such a busy job. Her particular line of runaways is young girls. People call her, both in the Police Department and out, reports the Brooklyn *Eagle,* "the mother of New York's disillusioned runaways." The runaway boys have a hard enough time of it, in many instances, but the real cases of misfortune and misery are to be found among the runaway girls, and it is such cases that fall into Mrs. Hamilton's special province. She has dealt with thousands of them in her career as a practising police woman....

Mrs. Hamilton was the only policewoman in New York [five years ago]. To-day there are one hundred and ten police and patrol women. And more are being trained as fast as they can be procured. So far most of the volunteers have been women over thirty-five or forty—mothers of growing families, women who understand the needs of the younger generation. But Mrs. Hamilton is hoping and praying that this won't be the case much longer. What she needs, she says, is young women. Girls who will go out among other girls, gaining their confidence and helping them to find their own. Girls who can better understand the point of view of other girls are better fitted to give real aid. And she's perfectly confident that it won't be a great while before she will be able to show New York and the world what a police woman really can do.

"There is too much restraint without intelligence in the home," says Mrs. Hamilton, "and almost every case that comes to our attention bears out this fact. A noted psychologist has said that crimes are often committed when a sex complex exists, that instead of normal self-expression a person will sometimes resort to an extreme activity even tho realizing that the act violates a law of society. I find this true in nine out of every ten cases I handle.

"New York is full of girls, well educated and of fair social standing in their home towns, who are simply down and out and too proud to write home and admit it. I can give you any number of examples. And, again, it is also full of foolish young things out for a thrill—mad to do something different, cause a sensation, make up for the colorlessness and uninterestingness of their lives—even tho it lands them in jail for their pains.

"None of them is vicious. They all just want to live. They came here with about five hundred dollars and a fair showing of clothes—according to home-town standards. They are going to enter college, work their way through. Or they are going into the movies. Or they are going to dance on the stage. Or they are going to make their mark in Grand Opera. Fine!—until they see New York styles. Their wardrobe seems somehow inadequate. Just a few new things will freshen it up a bit. And before they know it, between books and tuition at the colleges, or tramping about from one agency to another for the coveted front-row position in the newest musical comedy, or the lunches in the long waits for a voice trial before Gatti-Casazza, the small hoard is gone. They are absolutely broke. There is no one to turn to. No way of hoping for better things ahead. And write home, admitting defeat, they will not. They're just plain up against it. That's where we come in.

"We found two girls not long ago at one of the big department store's sample counter. For days they had been appearing around lunch time and trying all the samples. Nice girls they were. Well drest and of Southern extraction. They were so sweet and well mannered that the demonstrator hadn't the heart to turn them away. She fed them every day until the store detective 'wised' to what was going on. He called us in, and we took charge.

"They were refined, well-educated girls with unusually winning personalities. They had come from the South—the one to make her mark in the opera, since she was the best soloist in her home church, and the other to keep her company and rise high in the business field. Neither had realized her ambition. Both were absolutely broke. For two weeks neither had had a thing to eat except the salvage from the demonstrator. As I talked with them, the thinner of the two 'crashed.' Had to be rushed off to the hospital at once. Malnutrition, the doctors said. And she was a very sick girl. That's the one kind of case.

"For the other: three girls were arrested recently for shoplifting—college girls with plenty of money in their purses to pay for the petty articles they had stolen. And they were not victims of kleptomania, either. They had only taken the things for fun. Just for the thrill and excitement of doing something devilish and forbidden...."

Mrs. Hamilton leaned forward... and went on:

"It's so hard to do anywhere near all that's to be done with so few helpers. We need so many, many more. We want 'community mothers.' We want typing and stenography taught in the public schools. We want 'school advisers' in all the high schools, women to whom the girls may go with their psychological and sex problems. We want negro girls allowed in the telephone exchanges as the negro men are allowed on the police force. We want to teach hygienics to the poor. And I, personally, would like to see every rowdy, every bum in New York photographed, checked and put in bonds. Babies, I am positive, should be fingerprinted at birth. It's the only the right way.

"But how can we bring about such radical reforms without a suitable backing—without the understanding of the multitude?

"The problem of the prevention of crime is like a tin can tied to a dog's tail. And the police women are to the social problem what the nurse is to the medical problem. You've got to have us!"

The champion of right relaxed and smiled at her own vehemence.

"Oh, well," she deprecated, "you know how you get when you're terribly interested in anything. And I'm just living and eating and breathing this business. It makes me wild at the opposition we encounter. And each of us can do so very little. I'm doing all I can. But it isn't much. I bring home as many girls as I can accommodate every night, give them warm baths and good food, have their clothes washed and prest, and make them as comfortable as I can. Then I find them jobs and start in on a fresh bunch."...

"Only women can help women.... Do you know that 97 per cent. of the women tried are convicted without redress and there is no appeal from the woman's court? It's an outrage, and something has to be done about it. Isn't it time something drastic should be done?"

Mrs. Hamilton sighed.

"But I suppose I am too impatient. I want everything to be remedied at once. And the world isn't made that way.

"But it's bound to come eventually. And then the world will sit up and notice the police woman. That day can't come too soon for me!"

In 1925 Chloe Owings, a social worker who had been of service in various regions of the United States by that time and had also earned a doctorate in social service from the Sorbonne in France, emerged as an author as well. Her book, *Women Police: A Study of the Development and Status of the Women Police Movement*, was sponsored by the Publications of the Bureau of Social Hygiene and featured a preface by Lieutenant Mina C. Van Winkle, who had become the president of the International Policewomen's Association following Alice Stebbins Wells. In her preface, Van Winkle wrote, "The almost impassable gap which past prejudices have permitted to exist between the work of the police and all other preventive agencies must be bridged if we sincerely desire in the future to make headway in the struggle against delinquency and crime. The trained policewoman can and is furnishing this connecting link." The book endeavors both to cover the history of policewomen in countries around the world and especially to standardize terminology and methodology so policewomen can more effectively communicate and learn from each other.

Author's Note

BY CHLOE OWINGS

Women Police, 1925

As a social question, "Women Police" is as yet distinctly a movement with all the characteristics of a thing in motion and whose final direction and goal are not yet clearly conceived nor definitely formulated.

In no country, unless in England, have the various parts of this movement been correlated into a standardized formula. Within each country there are not only differences of opinion as to the basic utility or contribution of women officers of governmental departments and of private social agencies, but among these persons who advocate the appointment of women as police officers there are differences of opinion as to their functions, conditions of service, and the form of organization under which they should operate.

Further, not infrequently, two persons of the same country, both equally well informed, employ different terms in speaking of the same thing. It is difficult in the present phase of development of the

> movement to determine the exact meaning of terms used not only by persons of different countries but of the same country. It is reported, for instance, that the women officers in one city in the United States thought they were applying the "preventive and protective functions" as advocated by public service workers, when they "protected" the girls from arrest and then "prevented" her appearance in court, or her contact with other agencies, public and private, which exist to help her.
>
> This lack of standard definitions of terms with the exact equivalents in each of several languages handicaps discussion. The task of presenting a true picture of the movement is rendered more difficult when the only available information from most countries must be gleaned from the printed word, and particularly so, when statements by different persons concerning an identical subject are dissimilar. A correct interpretation of documents, letters, articles, and books written from various points of view and not based on a common acceptance of terms is very nearly impossible.
>
> This study attempts only to bring together between the two covers of a book the available information on the subject as a basis for study and reflection for those interested in the question.

Owings's book reflects the growing pains of the movement as policewomen in various locales implemented preventive and protective tactics as best they could interpret them. It also unflinchingly addresses the phenomenon of politics and prejudice preventing women from taking up positions of authority on police forces, and we'll continue to see this issue come up through the remainder of the policewomen and feminist movements to date, unfortunately.

The End of the Beginning

Also during this time frame, America's pioneer policewomen were moving toward the end of their careers.

Portland's Superintendent Lola Greene Baldwin retired in 1922, fourteen years after she first convinced the Portland mayor to let her launch the Women's Protective Division (WPD). During and after World War I, Baldwin served as West Coast federal supervisor, 1917–1921. She returned to the Portland Police Department for one year before retiring. Baldwin was also a member of the Oregon Social Hygiene Society and a special agent to six Oregon governors. She lived until June 22, 1957, active to the end.

Baldwin's friend and colleague Wilma Pearl Chandler Crounse, my grandmother, passed away in 1963 after a long life active in Portland's police department and community endeavors. Her colleague Myra Adams, who served on the women's association with Wilma, wrote to her family:

Everyone considered [Wilma's] work with the Women's Protective Bureau of great consequences and it gave her a type of experience and authority that fitted her well for her work with the Y.W.C.A. and interchurch civic activities. She was capable, poised though enthusiastic, a person everyone liked, a woman of firm convictions, yet agreeable to work with. In short, a very fine, unusual person and a wonderful friend whom we all loved and admired. It is no wonder she was sought after and that she occupied many important positions.

Lola Baldwin at age ninety-four. (Alfred A. Monner/*The Oregonian.*)

Over in Chicago, Sergeant Marie Connolly Owens retired in 1923 after thirty-two years with the police department. Her contributions to police work were largely unremembered to the public until the twenty-first century, but she was well revered in the Chicago police force. She passed away in 1927.

Alice Stebbins Wells, Los Angeles's renowned first policewoman, was the most visible of these early policewomen due to her national and international speaking engagements. In her final six years with the force, Wells was given the position of LAPD historian. She retired on November 1, 1940, after thirty years of service. Interestingly, Alice Stebbins Wells died on August 17, 1957, just two months after Lola Baldwin. Baldwin was ninety-seven and Wells eighty-four.

Through the years there have been numerous critics who felt it necessary to degrade or belittle policewomen's pioneers. Most of the scoffers give little consideration to the challenges these women faced in the forms of ridicule, scorn, and roadblocks from male police and city councils.

The early work of policewomen was not simply a battle between who was first, nor even who was the best, the smartest, the most glamorous, the one capable of using a gun, who wore her badge or a uniform, or who was the most highly paid. The experiences of Marie Connolly Owens, Lola Greene Baldwin, Alice Stebbins Wells, and many others provide evidence that there is more than one approach to helping women and children who historically were often not treated well. All three pioneering women fought great odds, succeeded in their work, and blazed the trail for coming policewomen.

Chapter 3
The Woman Citizen Series

Women's roles in America were changing rapidly in the 1920s. Women officially gained the right to vote in 1920, and across the country they were taking up jobs in record numbers, carving a place for themselves to become influencers and even leaders in society.

In 1917 suffragists combined various smaller publications and began publishing their news and calls to action in the journal *The Woman Citizen*, which came out on an almost weekly basis, circulated nationally, and continued publication long after women secured their right to vote. In 1924 the publication began to include a section specifically on policewomen. The series was sponsored by the International Policewomen's Association and the New York School of Social Work. The association was already proving to be a valuable resource to provide women with the training and standardization as Chloe Owings was calling for in her book as well as with resources to combat discrimination. The organization would grow in membership and visibility through the rest of the twenties, surely in no small part due to its series of articles in *The Woman Citizen*. The series focused on informing the public on the values of women police, the proper usefulness of policewomen, and the emergence of what by the late twenties was becoming a national as well as international movement.

While some of the articles in the series echoed topics and news like those shown in the previous chapter in other publications, their appearance in *The Woman Citizen* ensured forward-thinking women across the country were paying special attention. Furthermore, many of the articles in this series broached new subjects or discussed the topics in a novel way. This chapter chronicles several of the most prominent or poignant articles from that series to help paint the picture of women's roles in America during the 1920s and the growth of the policewomen movement during that critical time. Note that in the example below, as elsewhere, the author was unaware of the nation's first true policewoman. She mentions Portland, Oregon, without noting Chicago.

What the American Woman Thinks: A Policewoman's Life

By Valeria H. Parker

The Woman Citizen, June 28, 1924

The trend of recent public guardianship activities, just as that of public health programs, has been toward prevention. It is better in every way to keep a man well rather than to attempt to cure him when he gets sick. Similarly it is better—socially, morally, and economically—to prevent delinquency rather than to deal with its subjects. Both in medical and police circles it is still necessary to devote a large portion of the time and energy of our health and safety forces to salvage work, but the newer programs recognize more and more the value of preventive measures.

The rapid rise of the policewoman is gratifying evidence of her usefulness in the welfare efforts, as distinguished from the detective and arresting activities, of police departments. Though the policewoman movement is comparatively in its infancy, it already has been recognized as a strong constructive factor in the work of protecting society, not through the bringing of offenders to justice so much as through the adjustment of conditions which promote delinquency and criminality. The policewoman has a keen realization that "the way of the transgressor is hard," but her aim is to keep youth from seeking and finding that way. Through her sympathetic interest and understanding the right kind of policewoman is usually able to do this much more effectively than can her male co-worker.

Much of the lack of success which has been encountered in some cities is due largely to a complete misunderstanding of the policewoman's logical duties, and a failure to provide adequate training for her, or to secure the right type of candidates for the positions.

Raymond B. Fosdick, well known as an authority on police systems and methods, tells in this connection of his visit to one city where "the Chief of Police, in great bewilderment, was trying to teach his six new policewomen to shoot pistols—without great success—and to learn the intricacies of handling an eighteen-inch club.... When these accomplishments were finally acquired he intended to place the women on beats in precincts 'where conditions were not too rough.'" This incident occurred ten years ago, but there are still a number of commissioners and chiefs who hold somewhat similar beliefs.

It is recorded that, in the year 1903, Stuttgart, Germany, appointed a policewoman. Not until seven years later, however, does one appear in the United States—Los Angeles, in 1910, providing a policewoman to aid in safeguarding her public. Protective officers, however, were appointed in 1903 in Portland, Oregon. Since that date the rapid growth of the movement is indicated by the fact that approximately three hundred municipalities in the country now employ women in the field of public protection.

The problem of securing adequate personnel has been a most perplexing one. In some communities the police officials have selected their policewomen solely from the ranks of the widows of policemen and firemen. Their intentions probably are laudable, but many persons interested in public welfare have not hesitated to voice their disapproval of this method for qualifying candidates. Unless the woman selected has other qualities which tend to make her capable for the work it seems hardly fair, either to her or to the public, to assume that because her deceased husband happened to be a worthy and well-qualified public servant she will acceptably carry on the difficult and complicated task which is the policewoman's....

Although the duties of policewomen have been largely undefined and vague up to date, there is a general agreement among those close to the work that the best results are obtainable by organizing the women of a given police department in a single unit—a women's bureau or division—under the direction of a woman responsible directly to the chief of police. The woman in charge would be given a rank commensurate with the importance of her responsibilities. A questionnaire sent out in 1920 elicited responses from fifty-six cities having women police and it was learned that the policewomen in these municipalities were responsible to nineteen different authorities.

Tribute to the value and growing importance of the movement is found in the increasing attention given to it by universities and schools of social work. Among these are the University of California, the Boston School for Public Service, and George Washington University, Washington, D.C., which have planned special courses for women in the ranks. A comprehensive course for the training of police executives has been inaugurated in the New York School of Social Work. Here students receive their vocational training in connection with their full diploma from the School of Social Work. A limited number of scholarships for this course have been offered in the hope that women of high education and social standards may enter the course and qualify to meet the increasing demand for executives fitted to establish women's bureaus in the police departments of large cities.

The American Social Hygiene Association, a national voluntary organization whose program includes protective measures against sex delinquency, and law enforcement to deal with prostitution and other forms of illicit sex relationship, has cooperated in establishing most of the above courses.

Vassar and other colleges have invited lecturers from the Association to summarize for them the salient points in the policewoman's work and the distinct interest manifested by many of the students in these lectures points to an increased attendance at the institutions specializing in this field.

For the woman who seeks a career of service, who is willing to give the necessary time for adequate preparation, who realizes the difficulties confronting her but also appreciates the many opportunities for benefiting society as a whole, few openings exist which offer greater promise than that of the policewoman executive.

The Police Woman

By Katharine Bement Davis

The Woman Citizen, May 30, 1925

At the National Convention of the League of Women Voters held last month at Richmond, a resolution was adopted as part of the program of the Committee on Social Hygiene, calling upon women to work for the appointment of police women, and the establishment of a Woman's Bureau officered by a woman, in all cities in the United States which had not already taken such action.

There is significance in this because it reflects what is coming to be recognized generally: there is no more reason for putting women on the police force than there was in giving them the ballot unless they have a real contribution to make. This contribution lies in what can be accomplished in preventing delinquency and in giving greater protection to women and children.

Her Social Contribution

A survey of the history of the movement shows that not only in the United States but in other countries as well the appointment of police women has grown out of a need which could not be adequately met by private agencies. Although before the World War there had been considerable discussion and here and there a protective social agent had been given police power, or, more rarely a city had placed one or two women on its force, it was war conditions including the unprecedented and tremendous incursion of women into public life and business, that gave the great impetus to the demand.

It is interesting in this connection to learn that it was a war demand in France as long ago as 1356 which led to the first formation of a police force of any kind.

Policewomen, including Lieutenant Mina Van Winkle, head of the Women's Bureau, learn first aid from the American Red Cross in Washington, D.C. (*American Red Cross teaches Washington policewomen first aid work.* [Between 1909 and 1932] Photograph. Retrieved from the Library of Congress, <www.loc.gov/item/96514588/>.)

The earliest employment of women in this field in the United States was as a result of special circumstances or of special activities of women's organizations, as for example, in 1845, when the American Female Reform Society secured the appointment of six women matrons in New York City to serve at the Tombs and on Blackwell's Island in order that women convicted of crime might be cared for by members of their own sex.

So far as is discoverable, however, it was not until 1905, during the Lewis and Clark Exposition in Portland, Oregon, that a woman was put in charge of a competent force of social workers and given police power in order to deal effectively and directly with social conditions threatening the moral safety of young girls and women.

Twenty years later, we have police women on the force in at least 118 cities. Of these, 72 have appointed women since 1917.

The plan for the use of these women varies. In some instances they are distributed to the detective squad, the vice squad, the Bureau of Missing Persons, etc. In other cities, notably Washington, D. C., and Detroit, Michigan, they serve in a special Women's Bureau or Division, officered by a woman.

With the growing interest of organized women, there is shaping itself a formulation of the functions of women police which places greater emphasis on those forms of activity in which woman can supplement rather than duplicate those of her brother officers. The same tendency is exhibited in other countries.

In England as early as the eighteenth century the subject of women constables was at least broached, but distrust, apparently of her lack of the supposed necessary physical strength, prevented any action. A century and a half later, last year, the same view was expressed in a report of the replies of the mayors of a number of French cities to a letter asking their opinion as to the desirability of women police.

The successful employment of women to safeguard the soldiers on leave from the approaches of women of undesirable character and to save from danger the many young girls afflicted with war hysteria, quite converted large groups of English men and women to the possibility of using women on the police force for preventive and protective purposes.

In Germany, where the earliest tendency was to use women on the police force in connection with the regulation and licensing of prostitutes, sentiment among women is very strongly swinging in favor of their more hopeful and helpful use as protective and preventive agents.

In general, the women police themselves, particularly in the United States, have again and again expressed themselves as sanctioning that conception of their duties which embodies the socialization of their activities. By "socializing," we have in mind a broadening of the definition of police function for men officers as well, and Arthur Woods, former Police Commissioner of New York City, formulates this when he writes: "The preventive policeman is the policeman of the future." Through their own organization police women are trying to "put across" this conception.

Members of the International Policewomen's Association, 1925. (*International Ass'n of Police Women, 1/22/25.* Photograph. Retrieved from the Library of Congress, <www.loc.gov/item/2016839152/>.)

The International Association

The Association was organized in 1915 through the instrumentality of Mrs. Alice Stebbins Wells. Its original constitution set forth its standards at length, specifying among other things the use of police women chiefly for protective and preventive work, the employment of professionally trained women, the establishment of courses of instruction in universities or schools of social work, and the keeping of proper records. After ten years the revised constitution gives briefly as the object of the Association, "to fix standards for the service of police women, to secure the appointment of qualified police women, to encourage the establishment of women's bureaus in police departments, and to promote such service internationally."

The development of the organization has not been rapid. Its members have been women actively engaged in police duties, and up to very recently this membership has been confined to the United States and Canada. It's president since 1919 has been Lieut. Mina C. Van Winkle, than whom there is not a busier woman in the country. Its vice-president is Deputy Police Commissioner [Eleonore] Hutzel of Detroit, and its secretary is Ruth A. Sanders of the Police Department of Richmond, Virginia.

During the last year the Association has arrived at the dignity of a headquarters, a budget and an executive secretary....

It has an advisory committee of six, all of whom are women well known for their work in related social fields, and it is building up a council which is really international in character.

The call has gone out for the Annual Convention of Social Work, which is to be held in Denver, Colorado, for the two days preceding the National Council of Social Work, that is, June 8 to 10. An interesting program is promised which will well repay the effort to be present of any women interested in securing women police in their own community.

The Socialized Policewoman

By Dr. Mary B. Harris

The Woman Citizen, June 27, 1925

To clarify our discussion, let us explain what is meant by "policewoman"; and define the adjectives "socialized" or "socially-minded"—although we all vaguely know when we use these popular adjectives what they mean. Their root goes back to the Latin word for ally: and society is an alliance. A socially-minded person then is one who not only does his part toward the welfare of the alliance, and does it well, but who also sees his interrelation with the other allies, and that the alliance will be sound and prosperous in proportion as all the allies work together for its perfection.

Just what place in this alliance has the policewoman? The police [officer] is the official agent supported by taxes levied upon the alliance or society to carry out and enforce its will toward safe-living and uprightness. Its purpose, Webster says, is to detect and prevent crimes. Dr. Arthur Woods adds, "To prevent people from becoming criminals." In other words he humanizes or socializes Webster's definition. You will say that every educational and preventive agency comes under this broader definition. True, but only one is the universal, official agent—the police. Other agencies recommend. The police have the power of the law to execute their recommendations and orders.

Policewoman vs. Other Social Workers

Of this power the policewoman partakes. She derives her authority from the fact she is a sworn officer of the law, with all the power of a policeman—the broadest power (lawyers will tell you) that exists under our government. It is this which differentiates her from other preventive and protective workers. They act under moral obligation: the policewoman, under legal obligation as well. They may act, she must act.

With this definition clearly in mind, let us consider what functions of the police are as well performed by women as by men, or better. It is not only the right, but, by decision of the court, the duty of the police to be guardians of the safety of and welfare of minors; and this is one of the functions that can be taken over by the women....

To accomplish this task of protecting children and of dealing with all the women who come into the hands of the law, either as offenders or victims of offense, we believe that the policewomen should be organized into a distinct unit or bureau with a woman director ranking next to the head of the police organization. They should have their own precinct with proper detention facilities. They should either be summoned immediately to take charge of any woman or child coming into custody of the police or such cases should immediately be brought to the women's precinct.

Where the policewomen are not so organized, they do not function toward the prime object for which they are especially qualified, namely protective-preventive work for women and children, but are parceled out among the various precincts, where they are likely to be used as clerks, switchboard operators or matrons—any task that seems too slight to demand the service of a man. Thus scattered, they can never be a part of a comprehensive, constructive plan working toward the prevention of delinquency and the protection of women and children. This function must be emphasized, and their organization into a distinct unit as means to its fulfilment be insisted upon.

I mentioned the fact that policewomen might be used as matrons unless they were organized into a bureau. We are often asked what the difference is. A glance at the qualifications for policewomen set up by the police chiefs themselves will show the high standard that it is sought to establish for this service. A policewoman must be a graduate from a standard high school and have not less than two years' experience in systematic social service or educational work; or equivalent experience in nursing or executive commercial training. It is obvious that it would be economic waste to use a woman with the above qualifications as a police matron, whose duties are chiefly to keep the detention quarters clean and orderly and furnish chaperonage there and in court!

It may be asked how and where can the necessary training and experience be secured. There are several schools offering courses, notably Simmons College, New York School of Social Work, and George Washington University. The programs of these institutions show how comprehensive a background is desirable. This theoretical work should be supplemented by field-work, and by association with a good bureau, where the whole round of duty may be studied.

It is not easy to become nor to be a "socialized policewoman," but it has great compensations—not in money, although the salaries should average well with other forms of social work—nor in ease, for a conscientious policewoman knows no limitations of hours and time off. But those who have come to this field after experience with other agencies, find their satisfaction in dealing with a great variety of problems in an authoritative and effective manner; in knowing that they are dealing with fundamental misery in a vital way. As one policewoman said, "The service becomes your avocation, as well as your vocation."

Group portrait of policewomen, 1923. (*Police Women's group, 5/14/23.* Photograph. Retrieved from the Library of Congress, <www.loc.gov/item/2016834858/>.)

Essential Qualification

It is not a calling for the immature mind in an experimental stage, groping after its own philosophy of life. The policewoman must have her own standards high and firmly held. As this same policewoman said, "When a woman in agony begs you to pray for her, you can not wait to argue as to whether there is a God, or even to send for a clergyman. She needs help right then when the crisis comes."

In the light of all this, what does it mean when we thoughtlessly say that "children should not have to come into relations with the police"? Are we letting our old phrase becloud our vision of what the socialized police may become in the life of the community if the community holds them to the high potentialities of which they are capable? Let us beware of giving a bad reputation to our official, legally constituted guardians of morality, and allowing policemen to cloak their individual failures under the ill-repute in which the service generally may be held. The police will be of the quality that the community expects and demands—and no better. Let us read "socialized" into the word "police" and tolerate no other type of service. The "socialized policewoman" being new in the field is pointing the way.

Policewomen in Conference

By Mina C. Van Winkle

The Woman Citizen, August 1925

The Eleventh Annual Conference of the International Association of Policewomen as a kindred group of the big National Conference recently met in Denver, Colorado....

An interesting feature was the Joint Session with the National Probation Association. Four viewpoints for the care of difficult and delinquent children were presented: "The Attendance Officer," by Mr. Newton Hegel, Minneapolis; "The Probation Officer," by Mr. Baxter, Detroit; "The Visiting Teacher," by Miss Elizabeth McMechen, Berkley, California, and "The Police Officer," by Mrs. Mina C. Van Winkle, Washington, D.C....

Approved resolutions having general significance were in substance as follows:

1. To invite and urge the International Association of Police Chiefs to send delegates next year and to participate in the program.
2. To appoint a committee for the study of means of affording greater protection to boys and girls through more adequate patrolling of public parks and pleasure boats.
3. To oppose the distribution of obscene and salacious literature and to urge all policewomen to make a concerted effort to eradicate this evil.
4. To recommend that a National Bureau of Missing Persons be established in the Department of Justice.
5. After reviewing the film "Lilies of the Streets" it was unanimously condemned and the Secretary was instructed to notify the Police Department and the Women's Clubs of New York City that the film is a libel on good police procedure, police detention, the courts of the city of New York and upon the generally accepted preventive-protective service of policewomen.

If I Were a Policewoman

By Margaret Moss

The Woman Citizen, October 1925

"O wad some Power the giftie gie us
To see oursels as ithers see us!
It would frae monie a blunder free us
An' foolish notion."

The Scotch bard probably never heard of policewomen, but his immortal lines might well have been the motto of a policewomen's conference held recently at a state correctional institution for girls. Neither he nor any one of his day could have imagined a round-table discussion in which policewomen and officers of a correctional institution would sit side by side with the inmates themselves to discuss their common problems. These fourteen girls, apparently about sixteen years of age, representing the Student Government Organization of the institution, were all under court commitment to the care of the state until they attained their majority.

As "Ithers" See Us

The policewomen's problems had been acutely theirs, but we wished to make the discussion impersonal. "If you were a policewoman in your own home town, what would you do?" was the first question laid before these eager young things—

eager, partly because they were young, but largely because, as one of them confided to the superintendent, "There have been lots of conferences held *about* us, but we have never been asked for our opinions before." And opinions they had—valuable ones; and as the questions were asked, they gave thoughtful, well-weighed suggestions: suggestions as to what could be done to save other eager girls from making the mistakes that had darkened their youth.

"I'd see that there were more chances to have a good time in the right way" was the first answer given by a girl of about seventeen who seemed to be a leader, and who we were told was looking forward to being a trained recreational director. The others nodded approval; and as the discussion proceeded, urged playgrounds for the small children and clubs for the older ones as a means of providing good times.

"The ordinary right sort of good times aren't interesting," they said. "More girls go wrong because of uninteresting good things, which they desert for the more exciting forms of amusement, than from any temptation."

Problems of the small towns and big cities were discussed separately, but there was strong unanimity of sentiment for a wide variety of activities—outdoor sports, dramatics, dances, sewing classes, nature hikes "like we have here," Girl Reserves, Girl Scouts, Young Women's Christian Associations and literary clubs. The policewomen on the job should see that her community has these things, even if she has to start them herself.

The girls' club seemed to be the chief tool in a policewoman's kit. But how was she to get a girl whom she found slipping interested and into those clubs? Should she personally conduct her there and introduce her? "No, too conspicuous!" they said. "Better to get another girl to take her along, although it might be a good thing to notify the club leader privately." "Would the girl go?" "Sure; you've got to do what a policewoman tells you."

It was clearly recognized that a club's success depends upon the leader. She should be "full of pep" but have common sense, be attractive and have a "good enough reputation so she could be a chaperon without anybody saying anything." A club leader should have lots of ideas and, moreover, be able "to put them across the footlights." And to find the rare creatures who make good leaders, and get them to run clubs, was considered a legitimate duty of policewomen.

"The work of the policewoman should be taught to all school children." Ventured another: "She should get the churches to open their doors oftener than on Sundays and prayer-meeting nights, to make their services attractive, and to provide good times." Any Good Samaritan task was considered within the policewomen's sphere until the cooperation of specialized forms of social work for handling these difficulties could be secured. All this they said haltingly, feeling for words to express themselves.

"But aren't you *new* policewomen going to let us go to the dance halls and movies at all?" asked with mock dismay a slender little policewoman who appeared not much older than the girls themselves, though we all knew the conspicuously fine work she is doing. Back shot the answer from one of the delinquents: "Not *every* night and you must be home by eleven." Then opened the discussion of the dance halls, over which the entire group of girls shook or nodded their heads; they agreed that the danger was not all in the hall itself; but "when you come to go home."

Often it is so late that the girl is afraid to go home and does not know what to do. All agreed that policewomen should supervise dance halls, too, though not conspicuously. "There are a million ways a woman can scrape an acquaintance with a girl who needs help without attracting attention." A policewoman should also be on the Board of Censors of motion pictures—truly an idle life is not for her!

"Would you wear a uniform?" the girls were asked. Unanimously "No!" Said one: "I would wear my badge, a small one, like a frat pin, so that it didn't show. You can help a girl a lot more if you don't embarrass her." They were not sure they would like the term "policewomen," although they could not think of a good substitute. "It sounds too much like someone chasing you," hazarded a merry lass who looked as if a chase would be a lark for her. "Helping, not chasing, is what a policewoman should do"—to which one thoughtful girl added that she wondered why the same was not true of *policemen*, too.

"Do you think a policewoman can do what a policeman can't?" "They certainly can," was the answer, to which all thoughtfully again nodded approval. "Girls would much rather have a policewoman than a policeman talk to them. They would be willing to confide in her. Policewomen can help girls and keep them from going wrong so that they will not have to arrest them."

The Great Need

Over and over the need for help and friendship was brought out—the real kind that needs no label. "One thing I would never do if I were a policewoman," said one youngster, "and that is to say to a girl, 'I am interested in your welfare.'" It is a friendship that is deeper than words that these girls seek in a policewoman, and the policewoman will not go far astray if they see themselves as these "ithers" would like to see them. ❧

The City Manager and the Policewoman

BY LOUIS BROWNLOW

The Woman Citizen, November 1925

Recently a woman who was working to persuade the powers in her town to establish a Woman's Bureau in the Police Department came to see me.

"How shall we go about it?" she asked. "We have been talking for two or three years, but we don't get anywhere."

"Do you wish me to tell you the quickest and surest way?" I asked; and, of course, she became a living "Yes!"

A women's police bureau, ca. 1920. (*Women's Bureau, Police Dept. Photograph.* Retrieved from the Library of Congress, <www.loc.gov/item/2016852317/>.)

"Attend carefully, then, while I tell of the royal road," I went on. "Go back to your town. Get the women together. Organize. Plan. Get the men together and let them think they thought of the whole thing. And then launch a campaign for the council-manager form of government. If you win, you will get a city manager, and the chances are you won't have to ask him. He will start the movement for a women's Bureau and will be after you to back him up."

As long as she thought I was entirely serious she was grieved. Then she began to suspect that I was spoofing her and was gently sarcastic with me because I was placing first the extension of that form of municipal work which encompasses my profession, my vocation, my avocation and my mission; postponing in time and in interest her vital question. Yet I am not sure that my facetious reply was so far wrong. Often enough energy is expended in accomplishing one minor reform to bring about a council-manager form of government and the employment of a trained municipal executive.

What-Job-Needs-To-Be-Done

Such a revolution means a change of emphasis from Who-Shall-Have-This-Job to What-Job-Needs-To-Be-Done. And when this gets into the mind and heart of City Hall the next question is Who-Knows-How-To-Do-This-Job-That-Needs-To-Be-Done? A job that needs to be done is the protection of girls and young women. A woman knows how to do this better than a man. The job is part of the police work, but not one that has been well done by policemen. No one knows that fact better than a policeman—after he has seen a policewoman on the job. So, manifestly, if we are thinking in terms of getting the work done, we will want policewomen to do it. And we will want to give them all the authority that we give policemen, and all the machinery that they need, which means a separate bureau reporting directly to the head of the department and under the direction of a trained and qualified woman.

And Then What?

So, I say that the City Manager will establish the Women's Bureau. He will make a woman the head of it, to report to the head of the Police Department. He will give her a rank and title, and he will tell her to take her policewomen and Do-This-Job-That-Needs-To-Be-Done to stop delinquency among women and girls....

I am sorry I have not the statistics about City Managers and policewomen, and have not had time to send out a questionnaire. I have been City Manager of two cities, and in each I have established a Woman's Bureau. In Petersburg, Virginia, Sergeant Minnie Rowland is in command. In Knoxville, Tennessee, Captain Annette Steele is one of five police captains with equal rank and pay. In the annual convention of the International City Managers' Association, the work of policewomen has been an important feature of the program for four years and was given a major place in the proceedings in Washington in 1923.

I know of many cities where the movement for the establishment of Women's Bureaus has been led by the City Manager. In others, I know he has given instant support and, therefore, brought to successful conclusion a movement started years before his advent. The presence of a City Manager makes it easier for the women to get this important service started. Without [exact] figures, I shall not attempt to estimate the many city managers who have aided this advancement, since I might easily omit the best examples. However, since Cleveland, with its just under a million population, is the largest city that has adopted the council manager form of government, I may take that as one example and quote City Manager Hopkins:

“The movement for a Woman’s Bureau originated with the Women’s City Club. Assisted by Mrs. Van Winkle and Miss Hutzel, this club secured, late in 1923, assurance of cooperation from the City Manager and City Council elect. After the Manager and Council had entered office, this matter received active attention and resulted in an ordinance which designated the head of the Bureau as the ‘Chief of the Women’s Bureau,’ with the rank and pay of captain, reporting directly to the Chief so as to be under no necessity to confer with any of the inspectors and so to be absolutely free from interference by any officer in the department except the chief. After the ordinance went into effect, Miss Dorothy Henry, who had been strongly recommended by the parties most interested in establishing the Bureau, was appointed Chief and centered upon the work of gradually building up the department. Thus far, the number of policewomen is small, but provision is made for a larger number, and it is the policy of the department to build up gradually and with the most desirable material. Miss Henry’s word thus far has been gratifying in the extreme and has been a complete answer to the criticisms made in advance of the creation of the department and also fears as to this interference with other departments.”

Women’s Work

In Kansas City and Cincinnati, both large cities that have just adopted the council-manager form of government, women had the preponderant share in the revolution brought in the new government. I am sure that they will [get] to it in these large cities, as they have in many smaller ones, that the policewoman is given a full opportunity to demonstrate her great usefulness, her amazing zeal, her utter indispensability. ❧

From the Diary of a Policewoman

BY HELEN D. PIGEON

The Woman Citizen, December 1925

November 5th.

As so often happens when I am on night duty, I had to report at Court this morning and find myself at the mercy of a fifteen-hour day. Apparently, the police are charged with the administration of all the laws except those affecting their own hours of labor. But I was glad to have Margaret’s case settled so satisfactorily and it was funny to see the surprise on Police Officer Emery’s face when he heard the whole story. Last week when I found her with a sailor in a dark corner of the park at midnight and asked her to come to the Woman's Bureau with me, this officer was standing near and tried to persuade me to send her home. The sailor was funny, too—he looked at me so sadly, and said, "Oh, lady, weren't you ever young?" But I hardened my heart because I knew that neither of them had spent three years making investigations for the Protective Society and learned how fundamentally wrong things must be at home when a thirteen-year-old girl is picking up strange men—and sure enough, they were! A mother who hadn't been sober for a week, two sisters with illegitimate children, a brother in State's Prison and the child herself already initiated into sex experiences too sordid for words. Certainly she needed the protection of the Juvenile Court, which, as Dr. Van Waters said in "Youth in Conflict," "stands as nearly as possible in the spirit of a wise parent toward an erring child."

Social First Aid

So I made the complaint and this morning the probation officer added to the social facts, the results of the clinical examination—a mind normal but retarded, and a body undernourished and bruised with blows. Probation in that home was out of the question and she was a little young for the Reform School, so the State Agent from the Board of Children's Guardians agreed to take her for trial in a carefully chosen foster-home, with a kind woman who can give her the care she has never known and in time blot out the memory of these horrible experiences. Of course, the case isn't finished yet because there are two younger children in that home, but the State Agent will take that up right away. It's a fearful task, but I've known them to succeed, even in worse cases.

This afternoon I spent in the office dictating records and in the early evening I went down to North Street to tell Mrs. Johnson that the policewomen in Detroit had located her missing daughter in a lodging-house. While I was in the neighborhood, I stopped in at the Tivoli Dance Hall. Mr. Hill, the manager, used to be so antagonistic toward the policewomen, but now he understands our viewpoint and when I saw Marion F—, who is only fifteen and, therefore, under the legal age for admittance to a dance hall, he quite voluntarily called her aside and told her she must not come again. Poor child, she does love to dance and there is nothing in her neighborhood in the way of wholesome recreation. I often speak to the local Woman's Club and I must ask them to plan something for the youngsters down there. Mr. Hill asked me for some suggestions about his hall and is thinking of putting in a nice woman as hostess. He is so different from the manager at the Studio Dance Hall, who allowed every bootlegger, dope-vendor and prostitute in town to congregate in his hall. It took us six months to collect the evidence to shut him up, but the Chief of Police stood behind us like a rock and we finally did it. No community on earth has room for such a man, but so few of the good citizens really know he exists.

When I left the Tivoli it was time for me to go home, but just as I turned down Hunt Street, I saw the beginnings of a "pick-up." I was so tired that for a moment I was tempted to look the other way, but just then the light shone on their faces, and I recognized in the man Mike Brown, habitué of the lowest dives in town, and the girl was such a pretty little Italian, with all the promise of a lovely womanhood in her face, so of course, I had to interfere. When Mike saw me he melted away. He knows how much mercy the policewomen have for him and his kind. On the way to her home, Carlotta V—, confided that she had skipped out of her window when she was supposed to be in bed and asleep. Her mother, apparently a good woman, was born in Italy and has brought with her all the traditions of the environment in which she was reared. She does not understand the liberty of American girls. Carlotta, on the other hand, is American born, she has attended our schools, she works in a factory and she wants to spend her own money and choose her own beaux. The worst of it is that they are both right from their own standpoint. Carlotta, however, has lost faith in her mother and has decided to seek adventure wherever she can find it, and her mother has lost all her loving sympathy for Carlotta. A fallow field for trouble.

Just a Little Readjustment

Naturally, Mrs. V— was amazed to find that Carlotta was not safely asleep, and then she was angry—so angry that she decided on immediate punishment. Carlotta hid behind me and for a few minutes I was in imminent danger of receiving the beating myself. Fortunately, an older sister appeared and acted as interpreter while I tried to explain the situation. I left things much quieter but, of course, it will take time. Tomorrow I shall ask Miss Ferri, the Americanization worker at the Charitable Bureau, to help. She is of Italian descent herself. Mrs. V—should learn our language and customs and Carlotta needs a girls' club and some wholesome outdoor life. Just a little matter of social adjustment after all, so easy in the beginning but so hopeless when the damage is done!

And now to bed—I really believe I have justified my existence for today, at least, both as an individual and as a policewoman.

Compiled from actual cases handled by policewomen. ❧

Police—Before or After?

By Jessie D. Hodder

The Woman Citizen, January 1926

The coming of the policewomen may be looked upon as an inevitable tendency toward the resocialization of the job of policeman. It is fair to suppose that the police were our first public social workers, and they should never have lost that place. Their function was and should have remained constructive so that their activities might have developed along the lines of protection and prevention. Different branches of social service would then have been created, as the need arose, within the department of the central police ideal. Law might then have been interpreted as the servant of mankind and not its prod and lash. Unfortunately the police developed as the strong arm of government, with pursuit, prosecuting and spying as its focus, and thus crushed neighborliness from among its activities.

The spirit of neighborliness and the need of its expression can not be smothered in life; if government does not hold to it as its most precious lead to law and order, private agencies will be created to make the effort. Such agencies, however, are incomplete, because where the beneficent power of the law is needed they can not claim it as their own; it is not an integral part of them, it is a borrowed thing, inevitably smacking of coercion when used. It is into this gap that we see the policewoman stepping as the social service arm of the police job, humanizing the city and its relations to youth.

Needed: Social Service

Twenty years ago social service was created as a part of the medical work in hospitals. It had a hard struggle for a place and recognition until it demonstrated that it did not purpose to encroach upon the duties of the doctor or the functions of the hospital, but meant to socialize the undertakings of both. It showed how large a part of sickness comes from wrong social conditions or attitudes. It now has a permanent and vital place in the treatment of sick people.

Similarly, there is in the Police Department need of a social service function focused to bring into the work the element of prevention, protection, neighborliness and adjustment; it will in no-wise lessen the dignity of the police job or infringe upon it. It should lessen the amount of evil-doing by the positive process of teaching public opinion to understand its share in the prevention of public disorder; it would make adjustments, be an ally of good recreation, teach citizenship as the highest duty of us all. For instance—many of the problems brought to a reformatory are not criminal in the least; they are social maladjustment problems which a socialized police could solve. Others are defects in the problems of Americanization, which again a woman police would treat as a social, not a criminal, problem.

As an example—"X, seventeen, illegitimate, very beautiful, hungry for affection and really to belong to some one, was unhappy with a half-insane foster mother who constantly called her a 'bastard.' Jealous and treacherous, in a passion of misunderstanding the mother had the girl committed as a 'stubborn child' to a reformatory. The girl recognized her obligations to the woman who had taken her at birth from her own mother, but every time she offered affection or service her way and not as the foster mother conceived it to be due, there was a clash. This situation was known to the neighbors and to the police. Handled socially, two hopelessly incompatible people would have been separated, the girl's interests and capacities developed and the world would have been the richer. Handled from the law point of view, a criminal has been created. After release, she returned to her foster mother in an effort to show her good will and try again—failed and disappeared."

Those who are clamoring for the "treat 'em rough" methods for prisoners would do well to inform themselves of how many prisoners need never have been sent to court even, if our communities were intelligently socialized.

Anyone who has heard Mrs. Van Winkle tell about the Woman's Bureau of the Washington Police Department must be impressed with the multiplicity of social problems brought to the Bureau for solution, and the human place it fills in the community. That such work is not only vital in our community life but can only be completely done by a socialized police force with women as its agents, is clear.

Prevention

It is in her value as a preventive social agency that I see the greatest effectiveness of the policewoman, and in the faith I have that she will reinfect the police department with the social ideal that I hold the keenest hope. She will know the city by neighborhoods and serve it in small groups, making of us all allies of government.

If one's imagination is fertile as one reads the newspaper headlines, or hears of the complex moral problems arising in the schools, in the factories, in the dance halls, in the neighborhood, one is convinced that a system is wrong which has no workers whose job it is to help to modify and

A new officer is sworn in to the Washington, D.C., police department, 1920. (*Training a policewoman. The newest recruit to the District of Columbia's little band of sleuths female is solemnly sworn into her office by Edwin Hesse, chief clerk of the police department. Oct.* Photograph. Retrieved from the Library of Congress, <www.loc.gov/item/91796412/>.)

dissipate these dangers, rather than stand by looking on until the tragedy ripens to the full, and then brings in so-called "law and order"! To what purpose? It almost seems as if it were simply to clear the road to make space for others coming the same way! In medicine we have the district nurse for preventive medicine; a woman's bureau would do preventive, public morality.

Training for the Policewoman's Job

By Edith Abbott

The Woman Citizen, April 1926

It is impossible to discuss questions of training for any kind of work without first undertaking a "job analysis" of the work itself. In spite of the fact that readers of this page are already well informed with regard to the policewoman's work, one or two questions demand further discussion. In the first place, in spite of the name "policewoman" the woman officer does not and should not do the kind of work our police officers are actually doing. She is not "policeman" engaged primarily in detecting crime; she is a social worker engaged in the most difficult kind of public welfare work. She needs of course a badge of official authority, but the fact that our so-called "women police" do not even wear uniforms shows how far their activities are from those of the regular members of the police force. The women police are public guardians not in the technical but in the literal sense of those words. In her preface to Dr. Chloe [Owings's] new book, "Women Police," Mrs. Mina C. Van Winkle, President of the Women's Association of Policewomen and Director of the Women's Bureau of the Metropolitan Police Department, Washington, D. C., describes the policewoman's activities as "preventive-protective work" and lays stress upon the appointment of women with "broad education and experience in social work."

Thorough Foundation

The competent preventive-protective worker acting as a policewoman is really a social worker and needs the best training a good school of social service can give. Her work, of course, is specialized, as is the work of the prosecuting attorney, but the latter needs a sound legal education, not a specialized training course in criminal law. So the "policewoman" needs to be first of all in these days a mature woman with the liberal education of a university and the professional education of a good school of social work. She needs courses in family case work, child welfare, public welfare administration and the discipline of statistics and economics as well as courses in criminal law, criminology, and theory and practice in the narrower field of social hygiene and protective work....

The policewoman needs to be a person of liberal education and she must have up-to-date knowledge of modern methods of social work and of social welfare theory. It is especially important that the organization of specialized courts such as the morals court and the probation service be understood in their larger aspects. The history and theory of the social hygiene movement should also be thoroughly studied. While the work of the policewoman may seem to be of a "routine" character, she frequently has an influential part in the shaping of large social policies and she should be educated to play this part well. She has the chance to lead her community forward, but she can do this only if she understands both the theory of social progress, the lessons of the social experiments of the past and the goal of the future.

High Standards

The suggestion that women police should be university graduates may seem to be setting too high a standard for such work. But if we accept the fact that these women are to be competent social workers, it is necessary that they should also be university or college graduates....

The setting of high standards is a matter in which the universities, the professional schools of social service, and the influential women of the country must all work together. The duties of the policewoman may not be higher in type or more difficult than those of the policeman if the latter are properly understood, but the work of the policewoman certainly can not be adequately performed by persons who have no more education than most of the men now filling positions in the police department. We must see to it that the standards for men police are raised, but in the meantime there is every reason for starting the policewomen's service on this newer and higher standard rather than on the old and admittedly unsatisfactory one. ❧

From the Diary of a Policewoman—II

BY HELEN D. PIGEON

The Woman Citizen, June 1926

It does amuse me to find that there are still people who believe that a policewoman patrols a beat and proudly twirls a night stick. Yesterday a college girl who needed some data for Sociology IV made the Woman's Bureau "Exhibit A" in her tour of investigation and she was openly surprised to find that we didn't wear uniforms or manacle out prisoners. When she found that most of us were university graduates and that three held degrees from her own college, she was even more surprised, but a little doubtful of the honor conferred upon her alma mater. But after she had visited our sunny House of Detention and had seen the children sitting happily at their lessons under the direction of a teacher lent to us by the Board of Education, and had examined the sewing of the older girls, who are being taught by a volunteer, and had asked innumerable questions about each and every case, she decided that there really was something in this job of ours after all.

The Runaway

I think the case which really gripped her imagination was Harry Robey, a chronic runaway, ten years old and handsome as a young Greek God. The only person he couldn't win over to complete adoration is his stepmother, who secretly encourages his roving habits in the hopes that the police will have him sent away permanently. We found the poor youngster asleep on a park bench and when we learned of some suspicious circumstances in the family history we made a complete investigation. This, of course, included a mental examination which showed that he was a very bright and unusual child who must be given a chance. The Children's Mission has found just the right place for him in the country and his foster-parents are developing his love of home by giving him a plot of ground and some livestock. He now thinks of himself as a part of the "landed gentry" and while he occasionally runs away, as witness his presence today in the House of Detention, his average has been reduced from about eight a month to one.

When Miss Whiting, the college girl, found that the policewomen were responsible for conditions in the public parks and amusement places she begged to go along with me, so I took her on my usual Saturday night round. I wasn't going to spare her anything, so we went first to the Palace Dance Hall. For a few minutes this hall seems perfect, with its glistening floor, rose-shaded lights and wonderful orchestra (wonderful, that is, if you like what the King of Jazz Orchestra calls music). But after you become accustomed to the dim light you notice many coarse, brutal faces there are in the crowd, mixing at will with the fresh-faced, innocent youngsters. And if you are at all initiated, you know that the pallid, slender youth is Matt Pierce, who has been released five times this year by a lenient judge, after convictions for dope-selling; and that the stout, red-haired youth is Joe Myers, who has recently bought a yacht from the proceeds of his bootlegging. And as for Nellie Ryan, the striking little blond dancing with the young sailor—but then I hate to think that any woman has such a history.

As I explained to Miss Whiting, the manager of this hall is reaping a fortune and he refuses to listen to threats or prayers, because he has political backing. But at last the Mayor, after several scandals and a gentle reminder from the women's clubs that election day is not so far off, has agreed to revoke his license if the policewomen can prove that criminals are admitted with the manager's knowledge and that innocent youngsters are being led astray. For several months now we have been collecting this evidence and next week we are going to open the case before the Mayor. There really is no excuse for such conditions to exist in any city and I'm glad to think that the club women are really interested in these matters. It wasn't ladylike during the last generation and the destruction went merrily on.

Just before we left the hall, Mrs. Brown, the matron, told us that she had sent three girls home that night who were under the age limit, sixteen years, and, of course, she had been taking notes on a lot of other abuses. The matrons in our city are carefully chosen and appointed by the policewomen, although they are paid by the dance hall managers. It is really a fine system because we are able to choose nice, motherly women who create a wholesome atmosphere but who realize that they can be removed if they fail to report to us evil conditions.

A True Samaritan

Since life is made up of contrasts, and to prove that public recreation can be perfectly wholesome, I next took Miss Whiting to Riverside. This is a large park on the shore of the river, owned and run by a Mr. Wood and his two daughters. He entered the amusement world as a peanut vendor and he has put his whole heart and considerable creative ability into this enormous business. There is a beautiful dance hall, excellent music and five efficient floor managers who quietly but quickly stop any improper dancing. Bad characters are made aware of their undesirability and soon return to more congenial haunts. There are inexpensive bath houses, a picnic grove where whole families spend the day and a dozen other amusements. But best of all, I think, are the tiny swings and merry-go-rounds for children, where young people, forgetting petting parties and joy rides, stand watching for hours, lost in the eternal joy of childhood.

Of course, we do not have to patrol this park in order to enforce the laws, but the Woods have so much kindliness that they are always finding stranded girls and runaway children and sick babies for us to look after. Tonight they had located a runaway from Toledo for whom the whole country had been searching.

When we reported at the Bureau at midnight we happened to meet jovial old Captain Casey, who asked his usual question, "Did you get the city clean?" Thinking of the Palace, I gave him an emphatic negative, but my little college friend spoke up, "Maybe not, but she's rubbing out some spots!"

Compiled from actual cases handled by policewomen.

The Policewoman's Due

By Helen D. Pigeon

The Woman Citizen, August 1926

The "Woman's Bureau Bill," which seeks to establish the Woman's Bureau legally in the Washington Police Department, has been delayed in the Senate by the opposition of Senator King of Utah. But it was passed unanimously by the House District Committee after consideration on sixteen different occasions. What was there, you ask, so new, so controversial, about this bill that it demanded the attention of our Congressmen for such lengthy discussions? Nothing, we must answer, except the prejudices which always attach themselves to the entrance of women into a new profession, and the very general feeling, often subconscious, of dislike for all the activities of the police.

The Bureau was established in Washington eight years ago in answer to the desire which every conscientious city feels to care for its women and children, some of them delinquent, some of them hapless victims, but all of them in need of delicate social adjustments demanding tact and technical skill. And such a need inevitably spells "trained policewomen." Under the guidance of Lieutenant Mina C. Van Winkle the Bureau has attained an excellence which has been the inspiration of similar Bureaus throughout the world, but it has never been established by law. It exists on the sufferance of the commissioners. Usually they have been well disposed, but when they are unfriendly the mere struggle for existence handicaps the routine work.

Provisions of the Bill

To secure this legal sanction is the prime purpose of the bill, and in the District of Columbia, which is the stepchild of our Federal Government, such action must come from Congress. *No change in*

Portrait of Lieutenant Mina Van Winkle, president of the International Policewomen's Association. (*Food Administration - Administrators and Staff - Mrs. Mina C. Van Winkle of Newark, New Jersey, was president of Woman's Political Union of New Jersey 8 years now head of Lecture Bureau of Food Administration.* Retrieved from the National Archives, <www.catalog.archives.gov/id/31481065>.)

the present status of the Bureau is asked, except an increase in staff, and rank for the women equaling that of men officers in similar positions. It does, to be sure, outline the minimum Civil Service requirements, but they are those already in use by the Civil Service Commission, the results of years of painstaking thought and experiment. It further defines the functions, but again they are those already performed and are copied, almost verbatim, from the present police manual. Their inclusion merely prevents misunderstanding within the department and in no way extends the powers of the policewomen. In amending the bill, however, the House District Committee eliminated the Civil Service requirements and restated the functions in one short paragraph.

The policewomen are grateful to the members of Congress who gave us understanding and service.... But it was obvious in the public hearings and in the discussions among the members themselves that citizens do not understand the police function. They can not realize that the police power is the broadest in existence, that it has never been defined by any judge and its only limitation is "reasonableness."

For instance, a lawyer, a woman judge and the president of a welfare association objected to the paragraph, "Investigate neighborhood conditions, hotels, rooming houses, public dance halls, restaurants, cabarets, skating rinks, and other places of public assembly," on the ground that it endangered the constitutional rights of the individual. Yet even at the moment the police all over the civilized world were walking around houses to examine windows, trying store doors, dropping into theatres to enforce regulations, and in a thousand other ways "investigating" neighborhood conditions and individual concerns.

We found, too, that Adam's method of blaming Eve is still popular with his sex, and even affects bills in Congress! When the policewomen arrest certain men who threaten the safety of young girls, these "mashers" invariably retaliate by claiming that the policewomen lured them into a flirtation. This myth has grown to such an extent in Washington that it has taken on the guise of truth and it was so disturbing to Mr. Hammer of North Carolina that he, in company with Mr. Underhill of Massachusetts, delayed the bill for weeks. We are glad to say that Mr. Hammer was never able to find a grain of evidence to substantiate these charges.

Masculine Views

The masculine objection to the professional advancement of women spoke most loudly when Mr. Zihlman of Maryland eliminated all promotions in rank and even our friends failed to fight this issue. Yet the present rank of the Washington policewomen is less than that in cities half its size and offers little attraction to the ambitious woman. Another catastrophe threatened when Congresswoman Norton wished to place the policewomen in uniforms. This was averted by the prompt action of the Chief of Police, merchants and social workers who realize its danger to the protective work of a policewoman, by stigmatizing her charges and advertising her most confidential errands.

Portrait of Martha Randall, head of the Portland Women's Protective Division. (Berger Photo Studio/*The Oregonian*.)

This misunderstanding of the police department is characteristic of us as a nation. We do not sense it as an army protecting us from the enemy within as faithfully as our troops protect us from foreign enemies. Hence we cripple it, discourage it, and then speak slightingly of the havoc which we have wrought. In teaching our children an unreasonable fear of the "cop" we reap a hatred of law enforcement which foreigners are pointing to as a serious national fault.

What is the woman citizen going to do about it? Will she stand by her sister who pioneers in this new field? Will she do her part to bring honor and understanding to all work which is devoted to the protection and guidance of youth?

Policewomen on the Pacific Coast

By Imra Buwalda

The Woman Citizen, March 1927

Freedom! How we of the Pacific Coast revel in the term! Freedom to ignore the merely formal social conventions; freedom from the bondage of an icy winter and the heat of summer.

"Yes, and freedom to commit crime!" dryly comments a great criminologist from the East. ["] But," he added kindly, "you also have the freedom of social mind that permits you to experiment with new and strange methods of crime prevention. For after all, it takes much the same type of mind to organize a Juvenile Court as to commit highway robbery!"

Which perhaps, explains the fact that the policewoman's movement originated on the Pacific Coast. During the World's Fair in Portland, in 1905, Mrs. Lola Baldwin was given police power in order to meet the social problems which the Fair threw into sharp relief. In 1908, the Portland City Charter, incorporated this service as the Woman's Auxiliary of the Police Bureau, and it is still a definite unit in the department known as the Women's Protective Division. There are nine women—only recently called policewomen—headed by Miss Martha Randall, who is fortunate in having the support of the women of Portland, the churches and the press. Eugene, Salem, Astoria, Bend and Oregon City also have women connected with their police departments.

California claims the double distinction of having the first woman in a police department actually to be called "policewoman," as well as the first policewoman to be a college graduate and a social worker. Those of us who are fighting for this standard today look with gratitude to Alice Stebbins Wells who, in 1910, presented a petition containing the signatures of one hundred influential citizens to the Los Angeles Mayor, asking for her appointment as policewoman. She is still a member of the department, which now numbers thirty. About twenty of the policewomen are attached to the Crime Prevention Bureau, composed of men and women officers, and headed by a man. The rest are police matrons.

Many of the smaller cities in Southern California have at least one woman in the police department, as for instance Santa Barbara, San Diego, Santa Monica, Pasadena, Alhambra, Monrovia and Venice. San Francisco has three women in the Detective Bureau who have been serving for many years. The city charter specifically limits the number to three, but there is a movement under way to form a Women's Bureau.

Chief August Vollmer of Berkeley, California, 1934. (uclamss_1429_4367, *Los Angeles Times* Photographic Archives [Colection 1429]. Library Special Collections, Charles E. Young Research Library, UCLA.)

Berkeley deserves special note as the "home port" and the police laboratory of Chief August Vollmer, America's foremost police expert. As might be expected, he has a very special kind of policewoman in his own department, Mrs. Elizabeth Anderson Lossing, often called "the best-trained policewoman in the United States," and she is specializing in pre-delinquency!

Seattle, Washington, has had policewomen for a dozen or more years, organized in a Women's Detective Division, with an Advisory Council of representative women to assist in specific cases, in matters of policy and politically. For there have been political difficulties in the past, but now we are congratulating the Seattle Division on the election of Bertha Landes as Mayor, meaning, of course, that its hands will no longer be tied. There are also policewomen in Tacoma, Bellingham, Spokane, Yakima.

We may say then that the policewoman's movement is well established on the Pacific Coast. But the old social stigma attached to the term "police" has by no means disappeared. Men's and women's clubs are often prompted to ask a policewoman to speak, simply through curiosity to see what a "lady cop" looks like. We still need education among socially minded people—especially among other social workers, who are often a bit "up-stage" with the policewoman; we most urgently need standardization both of civil service requirements and of the proper functions of the policewoman, and we need recruits to take advantage of the splendid opportunity to train for this service in the department of Social Economics at the University of California, where the post-graduates and students may do their field work under Chief Vollmer. ❧

Counselors-at-Large

BY RUTH TOPPING

The Woman Citizen, April 1927

A pale-faced youth with weak, trembling chin stands before the judge. Beside him a tense little woman pours forth the story of her struggle to make him "a good man." Anxiously from time to time she scans the lad's face for some sign of final resolve, some outburst of assurance, but notes only weak remorse and hang-dog shame.

"Madam," from the judge, "how long has this boy been giving you trouble?"

"I couldn't say exactly, your Honor, because things have been getting worse all the time, but as long as ten years ago—and he'll be seventeen next Monday—he has caused me worry; lying, stealing, going around with bad boys; and now he is beginning to take things from workers in the shop. I'm afraid that soon he will be doing more desperate things, for he's so easily led. I can't do anything more with him; I want him put away."

"Do you mean, madam, that this sort of thing has been going on nearly ten years and now for the first time you ask help?"

"But, your Honor, I couldn't bring my son to court as though he were really bad. I always kept hoping that somehow he would change. I talked with him, punished him, watched him. I tried to get him to play with nice boys, but it's all done no good.["]

"Sad, unfortunate—probably unnecessary," murmurs the judge, as he signs papers committing the boy to the State Industrial Farm.

This well-intended mother is no startling exception. Like many others, she felt competent to deal with a small boy's misconduct, but by the time the problem was past her control it was equally past the control of others. She is not vastly different from people who consult a doctor when they are in pain instead of being examined regularly, or who try to combat a small blaze instead of turning in an alarm before it gets beyond control. The evidence in these cases of incorrigibility demonstrates that we must find, early enough, those parents who, if not helped, will finally take their children to court. We must detect incipient delinquency long before the judge's, "Too late."

Intelligent, well-informed parents are rapidly learning the significance of certain types of conduct and are seeking professional advice on persistent naughtiness almost as readily as on physical ailments. Others, less intelligent or less informed, fail to realize the connection between defiant attitudes, deception, excessive day-dreaming, tendencies to bully or to avoid other children, and certain emotional disturbances which may induce such behavior. While these traits are by no means the invariable precursors of a criminal career they do mark a tendency to uneven or abnormal development that may find ultimate expression in an eccentric or inadequate personality, neurotic conditions and, in extreme cases, delinquency and insanity. Far removed from one or another as these results may appear, their earlier symptoms are in childhood indistinguishable. When this fact is more generally recognized we may have fewer organizations which seek to combat or prevent specific ills and more which strive to promote in childhood the fullest and richest individual expression and development that is compatible with group life.

Obviously the court may not engage in this task, since it plays the more passive rôle of receiving persons sent by others—the police or private complainants. The needed link between court and community is being increasingly supplied by women's bureaus in our police department. Women police definitely committed to the ideal of protective work and the prevention of delinquency, occupy a strategically favorable position for this very service. They have the weight of public authority, they can move about in the community, make their observations and take the initiative without waiting for the case to come to them. Thus they enjoy certain distinct advantages over private agencies, as well as over the court. Their training in high standards of social work renders them competent to detect and diagnose early symptoms of maladjustment and to refer families or individuals to the agencies or institutions best fitted to their needs. Their title may have something of a past to live down. Like the character in Alice in Wonderland, who made words mean what he meant them to mean, it is in their power to determine the connotation of "policewoman."

With the increasing complexity arising from specialization in all sorts of professional service the community stands in distinct need of some one to interpret and direct. Many people go to court with problems that belong more properly in a clinic, or seek from the court service better rendered by a private agency or institution. Where the policewoman makes the preliminary investigation of court cases, she may advise the use of community facilities and so avert the unnecessary stigma attaching to a court record. Parents frequently take their children to court where they are stamped as incorrigibles or runaways, when they themselves may be far more culpable. An unprejudiced observer might wonder why, in a country that boasts children's courts, so many children between sixteen and twenty-one are arraigned in courts for adults, where "justice" ranges itself, too often, on the side of parents, who, by mismanaging their children from infancy have provoked the very reactions which they condemn. The policewoman, occupying an outpost in the community, may often forestall such drastic steps, and, as her aims are better understood, become a counselor-at-large, able to deal with maladjustments in the incipient stage.

One Thousand Sponsors

By Helen D. Pigeon

The Woman Citizen, May 1927

With Lady Astor as Chairman, the International Association of Policewomen is organizing a group of one thousand sponsors, laywomen of prestige and proven leadership in all parts of the country. A definite quota is assigned to each state and on the initiative of the state chairman the sponsors are brought together once or twice a year at informal gatherings, at which the work of the policewoman is presented by a qualified speaker. Through these meetings and through the literature published by the Association, these sponsors thus become acquainted with the true meaning of the policewoman's service and form an important lay membership in promoting the educational program of the Association. It is part of this program to stimulate the appointment of policewomen, to educate public opinion, to give technical advice and field service to public officials, to collect data and by all other means to secure high standards of service from the policewomen and sympathetic support from the citizens. The sponsors are asked to contribute a certain sum each year toward this program and it is hoped that in time they will feel a new interest in their local police problems, and will lead the way to higher standards and greater efficiency in that rather neglected field, the prevention of crime. Eventually a similar group of men advisors will be organized....

The need for properly qualified policewomen is real. They protect women and children from the temptations which civilization is creating faster than we have learned to control them; their skilled adjustments in the cases of boys and girls avoid the humiliation of arrest in countless cases; and their constant supervision of places of public recreation, during the hours when other agencies are off duty, is a vital factor in the prevention of delinquency.

Humorists to the contrary, woman is just finding her voice. A taste of her new power as "the hand which marks the vote" has lured her into corners and crevices of our civic life which never knew her touch before. True to the form which once made her murmur over her bachelor friends, "He needs a wife," she has now issued an ultimatum to certain city departments which are charged with housekeeping and child-protection on a large scale. The public scarcely believed her when she said the police department needed women, but the courage and self-sacrifice of a few pioneers have extended the field to more than two hundred cities in the United States. That a woman's place may be in the police station is proved when every hour of the day and night brings its grist of runaway children, destitute children, sex delinquents and deserted wives, all in need of a guiding hand.

Personal, daily service of this sort is impossible for many women, but through their local clubs and civic groups they have given it strength and spirit. Sometimes they have been the initiators of the service; again they have saved it from the knell of political interference; always they have made their voice heard in asking for better facilities and finer standards. The organization of one thousand sponsors as a lay membership brings this sympathy into a more tangible form, to the advantage of the central educational agency which promotes the movement, the International Association of Policewomen; to the policewomen themselves, who do not profit financially of course, but who reap the benefit of a better understanding from the representative citizens of their state; but, most of all, to women and children who are deprived of the protection and the joys of the more happily born. ❧

The Policewoman and Deportation

BY JANE PERRY CLARK

The Woman Citizen, June 1927

If a girl, brought to the United States from England at the age of two, becomes a prostitute at the age of twenty, she is deportable to England and she becomes a grave social problem for both countries. The policewoman who comes in contact with her touches a question of international importance, and by realizing that her service is not confined to the limits of one community makes a real contribution to social work from the international point of view.

The United States has improved the machinery for administering its immigration policy so there are now few immigrants who journey to this country only to be turned back or excluded. There are, however, many foreigners living in the country who can be expelled or "deported," as it is technically called. We are now deporting each month about a thousand aliens, undesirable according to the immigration law. In the opinion of the Commissioner General of Immigration, deportation is one of the most important functions of the immigration service.

There are so many social problems involved in deportation that social workers and policewomen need to know about the law and how it works. Aliens may be deported within three or five years after entry, or without time limit at all, depending on the cause of deportation. Of most interest to policewomen are the last class, for among those who can be deported without time limit are criminals, prostitutes, white slavers and those brought to the country for an immoral purpose.

International Aspects

Deportation, in its procedure, is purely administrative, centralized within the Department of Labor, with the Secretary of Labor as final authority. Not a punishment for crime, it may be carried on without the safeguards of criminal procedure. The individual in question is reported to the local immigration official, who investigates, and if he finds grounds for deportation, applies to the Bureau of Immigration for a warrant of arrest. When this reaches him he holds a "hearing," at which the alien may have a lawyer and show cause why he should not be deported. The record of the hearing is then sent to the Bureau, where it is gone over by a board of three persons, who recommend that the warrant of deportation should or should not issue. The final decision is left to the Secretary or one of his assistants.

Application must next be made for a passport and in this we first see the question of deportation internationally. The United States may legally send out undesirables, but the countries to which they go may refuse to take them and an international *impasse* results. Where a man expatriates himself by a long absence from his country and has not become an American citizen he is a "man without a country." People may have citizenship different from the country from which they came; thus a Czech living twenty years in the United States, and there married a Cuban, on becoming insane cannot be deported to Czechoslovakia but must needs go to Cuba, where she has never been since she has become a citizen of Cuba through her marriage. A girl born in Germany of Austrian parents takes the citizenship of her parents, and if deported with tuberculosis, goes to Austria. A Russian may not be deported at all, as the United States has no diplomatic relations with Russia and no passport can be secured.

When the deportee reaches home he must begin life anew. The social problems which have caused his deportation do not end with his departure from this country and may be intensified by his arrival in a different environment. The policewoman must look beyond the confines of one country and seek adjustment from the international point of view. Although she by no means advises the retention here of those who are socially undesirable, she realizes that deportation may be merely passing the problems of one country to another, as we used to pass them from one town to the next, and there must be international cooperation in effecting a solution.

Two Points of View

The policewoman is in a position of peculiar vantage in that she is a public official as well, and can see the question from the point of view of official interest in public policy and from the standpoint of solving the problem of the individual. She is especially concerned with delinquency and its prevention, and is more apt to come in contact with the deportation of delinquents than is anyone from a private social agency. She it is who must look ahead to see that provision is made for social care of the person deported on moral grounds since the deportee is often entrusted in her custody while awaiting deportation. We may look to the policewoman as a liaison officer in the building of international machinery by which officials of different countries will one day cooperate in the care of their socially inadequate. ❧

In the late 1920s *The Women Citizen* faded as other national publications such as *National Municipal Review*, *Ladies' Home Journal*, *The Journal of Criminal Law*, and *The Annals of the American Academy* and more began to pick up women's news. Of note is the article "The Policewoman of Policewomen" that appeared in *Ladies' Home Journal*. The first page chronicles the early life of Mina Van Winkle and how she came to be the superintendent of the Women's Bureau in Washington, D.C., and the president of the International Policewomen's Association. Then the author applies a broad lens on the work of policewomen, excerpted below, which furthered the message that had been laid forth in *The Woman Citizen* series.

Lieutenant Van Winkle in her uniform. (*Mrs. Van Winkle.* Photograph. Retrieved from the Library of Congress, <www.loc.gov/item/2016828593/>.)

The Policewoman of Policewomen

BY ALICE AMES WINTER

Ladies' Home Journal, July 1927

Out into Busy Places

...When the war was over Mrs. Van Winkle found herself deep in a burning question: Should the District of Columbia, now her home, establish a Bureau of Policewomen? Other cities had been trying out women in various capacities as helps the police.... But the word "policewoman" still sounded queer and dubious. "Policewoman? Pound the pavements? Dip into dives and rub shoulders with filth and lawlessness? You can't get decent women to do that kind of work. Such women would themselves have to be streetwalkers." It was a case of push and push. The then superintendent of the District of Columbia was a journalist and not a dyed-in-the-wool trained policeman, which perhaps had something to do with his unconventionality of outlook. He wanted women. So a little squad came into authority.... Mina Van Winkle became so interested in their success that she volunteered to do the dreary and monotonous office work for a time.

It was not long, however, before she found herself director....

Law and Social Service

This new public servant, the policewoman, must blend the law and the gospel of social service.... For women and children she does what it is hard for men to do. She is the friend with the power of that young girl who looms before the eyes of all of us shivering on the brink of catastrophe. She goes along the street and into the place of commercial amusement with her eyes open, wherever young things congregate and wherever they need a wise friend and a wary one who knows the cunning ways of evil and knows its end, where youth sees only its tinsel beginnings. She cannot, like the philanthropist, reckon her doings in numbers of garments or meals given out, nor can she according to her professional ethics, flaunt her record of "cases." Reticence is courtesy toward those who have stood on the brink of the law but have not stepped into the abyss.

Nevertheless, kindliness and an understanding admonition that has in it no sting are her weapons. Only she knows that Mary Brown, after a few words, does not make a second venture in "pick-up" acquaintance.

Of course it took time. In a charming apartment in Washington, Mrs. Van Winkle sits and tells all about it—sits with glowing eyes, as one who is filled and overflowing with her beloved topic. Around are many books and pictures and comfortable chairs; all the atmosphere suggests delightful and leisurely home life. But, as Emerson [once] said, "Do not be deceived by curls and dimples. I tell thee that babe is a thousand years old!" This is the president of the International Association of Policewoman. Perhaps you did not know that there were enough of them in the world to form anything so august as an international association. You begin to realize it when she pours out the story or stories that touch tightly here and there.

The use of women, particularly in the protection of women and children, like most significant movements, is being worked out independently in land after land. Germany learned a great deal, just as we did, during the war, about how vice sinks into crime and how both undermine manhood and womanhood. Protecting women and children is also protecting young men and national vigor. England and the Continent, and even far-off spots in the Orient and the islands of the sea, are echoing the same need and the same solution....

Each has a story of its own that Mrs. Van Winkle would like to headline, though the general public in city after city is not very aware of this public servant, for the policewoman is not often seen in the glory of uniform. She wears quiet, inconspicuous dress as she goes about her work.

Protective Interest

Let one of them speak for her fellows: "The policewoman must walk the streets where the bright lights, jazz bands and the atmosphere prove to be so alluring to the very young girl. She must watch out for this young girl and apprehend her when she first plays truant from her work or school to go to the moving picture or the dance hall. She must locate the large group of children that are to be seen on the streets begging, and bring about the social treatment needed in these cases. She must be on duty at night observing upon the streets and in parks, watching out for the runaway girl, the streetwalker, and the commercial woman who solicits her trade on the public streets. She must be friendly and helpful to the unfortunate drug fiend and derelict and to the forlorn outcast who walks upon the streets."

You and I whisper to each other, once in a while, the story of one simple girl who disappears mysteriously and is not heard of again. Our eyes grow with big with horror and pity. What has become of her? Ask Mrs. Van Winkle about her. She will tell you that over twelve hundred girls were reported missing in the District in a year, and that more than a thousand of them were found.

Eleonore Hutzel, deputy commissioner of the Detroit Police Department and director of its Women's Division. (*Miss Eleonore L. Hutzel, 1920.* Photograph. Catalog Number 2011.004.204. Detroit Historical Society.)

> And because she is stretching her protective interest far and wide she may go on to remind you that this is not an exceptional thing but that it happens to both city girls and to young things who come in from the country and just evaporate.
>
> When women and girls are brought into court for trial, sometimes in cases that overwhelm them with shame and silence, a woman friend ought to stand beside them. Isn't Mrs. Van Winkle right? This is one of the offices of the new kind of officer in petticoats. Time was when it used to be said that no one was so hard on an erring woman as a good woman. But the last generation has changed that. A kind of gentle understanding and loyalty of woman for woman has sprung into being, a yearning and extended motherhood that stretches out wings of protection to its own who are in danger or have gone astray. Put that in official position, and you have the policewoman.
>
> Sometimes heroism of the kind from which a woman would most shrink becomes the plain duty of our policewoman....
>
> There is no closing hour to the kind of devoted heart that is called on for this service. It must be awake most when the world is dark. When the rest of us go on holiday, its work grows heavy. Any time the telephone rings, day or night, it must leap into action. Its emergency readiness reminds one of a doctor's. In fact, it is a doctor, a doctor of the soul of ailing women and girls, and a doctor of the modern school who cares more to keep us well than she does to heal disease. Let no woman seek this job whose idea is to limit her self-giving.
>
> Of course in enlightened spots the same type of farsighted, whole-souled service is being called for from men who would belong to "the finest"; and the two kinds, men and women, work together as men and women ought to work.

The 1920s were closed out with an article titled "The Policewoman" written by Eleonore L. Hutzel, deputy commissioner of Detroit, and published in *The Annals of the American Academy of Political and Social Science*. Its audience was more scholarly than that of other articles featured previously, with Hutzel including more statistics and data regarding the policewomen movement to date.

Most importantly, Hutzel dared to analyze the many issues involved in combining male and female police officers. "These problems are due, first, to the fact that it has been difficult to fit women into a well-organized military system developed for and by men, and second, to the fact that the appointment of women officers in a police department has, in almost every case, been a first step in preventive protective work. Thus the difficulty of bringing women into a men's organization has been aggravated by the new type of service which they have introduced." She called on chiefs of police to take the lead in showing acceptance to the new services and policewomen, saying that others in the departments would follow suit. "From an appreciation," she wrote of departments where this kind of leadership models tolerance and progress, "on the part of each group, of the contribution which the other group offers has come mutual respect and an improved police service."

The 1920s were no doubt a time of growth and progress as well as challenge for policewomen across the country. But the 1930s would prove even more challenging.

Chapter 4
The Depression Era

Despite all the progress for women, particularly policewomen, in the 1920s, the Great Depression shifted Americans into survival mode. Feminism and the police focus on protective and preventive work were no longer priorities. As authors Susan Ehrlich Martin and Nancy C. Jurik describe in their book *Doing Justice, Doing Gender*:

> Women's inroads into policing came to a halt during the 1930s. Hiring was frozen during that decade. Moreover, the crime control model of police work, which viewed officers primarily as soldiers in a war against crime, almost totally eclipsed the crime prevention model. The crime control model, fostered by J. Edgar Hoover and the FBI at the national level, centralized control and adopted a military-style command structure to address police corruption. The crime control model also firmly reinforced male, working-class culture and values in police departments and reaffirmed the superiority of the masculine virtues of the fearless crime fighter who is able to overcome resistance.

The Depression led to a lack of jobs in virtually every corner of the country, and crime levels increased nationwide, presumably due to people's desperation. President Herbert Hoover gave police forces permission to fight crime more strictly, and before long, the compassionate handling of delinquents and the system for preventing crime, which policewomen had advocated so strongly for, were things of the past.

The National Center for Women & Policing adds:

> **A History of Women in Policing**
>
> National Center for Women & Policing, 2013
>
> In the 1930s with the Great Depression came changes in how employment was popularly viewed, and women's [employment] suffered because of this. A married woman with a job was seen as

wrongfully taking a job away from a man who needed it to support his family. Women were always assumed to be on their way to getting married, if they were not already married, and therefore not needing a job. As jobs became more scarce, women's career aspirations suffered. This time period also saw a change in how law enforcement officers perceived their social role. In the mid-1930s the FBI was formed, and law enforcement officers began to project a role of "combatant of crime," turning away from the idea that police should work as social agents against moral decline or destitution. ❧

Author Erika Janik explains the state of the police force for those women who did want to continue.

From Mothers to Crime Fighters

By Erika Janik

Pistols and Petticoats, 2017

Some women found positions as part of crime-prevention or juvenile delinquency-prevention bureaus, which formed on the assumption that delinquency posed a major threat to cities, particularly during times of economic crisis. Policewomen generally opposed these units because women were not in charge—most fell under the jurisdiction of male officers—even though these units provided most of the job opportunities for women. Chicago, which had ignored demands to create a separate bureau for its women officers for decades, succumbed to the recommendations of a reform committee and established a crime-prevention bureau in 1931. As a result, the number of policewomen in Chicago actually increased, from 30 in 1929 to 61 in 1938, at a time when numbers elsewhere had ground to a halt or declined. Crime prevention received far more attention from reformers and community leaders than within police departments, however. Most of these units had few male officers and were composed primarily of policewomen. ❧

While it became harder for new women to enter the police field, existing policewomen dropped off drastically too, whether due to layoffs or because of a moral objection to the shift in the perspective of police work. The International Policewomen's Association faltered during this time too, becoming what the organization's website called a "Depression casualty" in 1932, which left even fewer resources for the policewomen who remained.

On the Policewoman's "Beat"

BY JOSEPHINE NELSON

Independent Woman, May 1936

Paradoxically, women have been admitted to that male domain, police work, primarily *because they are women*. Had a uniformed man approached Sophia, barely 14, when she was loitering at Broadway and 23rd in New York one midnight he might conceivably have frightened her into a lie and the car of the man who had been driving round and round the block—in low gear when he passed her. But a policewoman learned that she had run away from a small Pennsylvania town, sent her to respectable lodging for the night, and back home in the morning.

This same woman got the confidence of a girl whose sex delinquency had become the despair of her parents and uncovered facts about her criminal associates that led to three arrests, and eventually to the girl's social and economic adjustment.

One can readily see that it is easier for a policewoman than a policeman to apprehend shoplifters (a large per cent of whom are women); to patrol dance halls and see that decent standards of conduct are maintained. The child victim of rape, the boy who has been snatching bananas from a huckster's cart, the prostitute, can be interviewed more effectively by a woman than a man. And so it goes.

The instances suggest a long list of police situations in which women, as women, are genuinely needed. They also point to the fact that the policewoman movement had grown up as a sort of twin to the conception that intelligent efforts to safeguard the public must, more and more, lap over into the preventive and protective—that a myopic focus on the purely punitive is a hopeless treadmill. Police now know they must understand and cooperate with social agencies, regardless of just where they draw the line on actual participation in welfare work. And social welfare has always been preëminently [a] woman's field.

Many things have happened since 1910 when Mrs. Alice Stebbins Wells, graduate theological student and social worker, induced a hundred influential citizens of Los Angeles to sign the petition that secured her appointment as a police worker, the first bona fide "policewoman" in the United States. Pioneer Wells is still on the job. She recently established and was made curator of the Police Department Museum in Los Angeles. But by her side, figuratively, there are today an estimated 850 women police in 290 American communities.

It is extremely difficult to draw any composite picture of the American policewoman, for there is no central clearing house of information about her. Even numbers are hazardous. With each local government, each county, each state developing its own police force and defining its own terms, generalization becomes a kind of conundrum: "When is a policewoman not a policewoman?" Sometimes she bears the name, but is simply a matron supervising or serving women and children in police custody. And we have had matrons since the American Female Reform Society secured the appointment of six in New York City in 1845. Often one woman may combine the duties of protective officer, matron and even detective.

The set-up under which she works varies widely. Some of the larger cities have women's bureaus headed by a woman of experience and rank; sometimes the head is a man. In far more places there is no woman's bureau, and policewomen are assigned to different squads or bureaus.

By and large, however, the American policewoman is a social worker with police powers, rather than a detector of crime. She handles a 32-calibre six-shooter expertly (several women score 95 at monthly target practice in New York), but she seldom carries the thing. Of the entire woman's force of 150 in New York, perhaps three habitually have revolvers in their handbags—"One simply doesn't need a gun." One needs, rather, a knowledge of human nature and quick wits, and perhaps—on precinct duty—a nursing bottle for stray babies and a first-aid kit. Though it must be admitted a gun came in handy the other day when Patrolwoman Alice Shanley of the New York pickpocket squad apprehended two burly suspects at the same time. Some policewomen are police officers primarily; most are social work experts.

Almost never is this American policewoman uniformed. New York's force last summer acquired blue serge outfits with brass buttons and overseas caps, but they rarely are worn except around prisons and occasionally on Coney Island beach patrol, where an agglomeration of foreign elements makes visible authority desirable. The policewoman is as nearly a perfect physical specimen as may be, though emphasis is more on brains than on brawn. Her intelligence quotient is high—one tenth of New York's force are college graduates. Though England's policewomen lose their jobs if they marry, America's usually have husbands and often children. To cite New York statistics once more, only seven of the 150 are single.

You will find the policewoman (*if* you find her, for she is far from conspicuous) patrolling public dance halls, visiting motion picture houses, railroad stations—any public place where conditions that contribute to the delinquency of boys and girls may be found.

Appointment of policewomen has been promoted by the United States Children's Bureau, American Social Hygiene Association, National League of Women Voters, General Federation of Women's Clubs, and innumerable local women's clubs and social and civic agencies. The movement received great impetus during the World War years, to combat the evils which grew up in the neighborhood of camps. And numbers of policewomen increased greatly after the close of the war.

But what of the present and the future? Indubitably the depression's tightened purse strings have halted expansion. Baltimore, where the law permits not more than five policewomen, has not filled a vacancy caused by a retirement several years ago. New York with the largest women's force in the country and the largest the city has ever had, has made no new appointments in four years. The situations are fairly typical.

Can, then, police departments of tomorrow offer vocations or careers to more women? Will those already in the work continue to be assigned chiefly to women's and children's cases, or will new doors open to them? Opinions vary greatly, but the majority of officials in the seventeen cities that provided Independent Woman with information were optimistic.

"I am of the opinion that policewomen will in the future do many things in police departments which they are not doing today," said Miss Eleonore L. Hutzel, deputy commissioner of the Detroit Police Department and director of its Women's Division (thirty-nine policewomen, three women sergeants, and three men detectives work under her).

"Without question there is a place for women in the various fields of detective service. Those going into this work, however, will need a different type of training from that of the policewoman in the protective field," thinks Miss Hutzel. "On the other hand, the work which women can do will always be minor as compared with what men can do. But the general feeling among executives in the Detroit Police Department is that policewomen are an essential part of every well-organized police division, and that in Detroit we could not do without them."

George T. Ragsdale, superintendent of police training in Louisville, which has four policewomen, declared, "I can see a great many places where women might be used. There is no reason why they should not perform certain phases of detective work. I think most of the clerical work could be better performed by women. There is no reason why the pawn shop and modus operandi bureaus should not be headed by women; why women should not take finger-prints and classify them as well as men. In fact, the general rule that a person should be permitted to work wherever ability commends her should apply to women as well as to men."

Sergeant Rhoda Milliken, head of the Women's Police Bureau in Washington, D.C. January 3, 1933. (International Newsreel Photo. Courtesy Richard Lake.)

Less specific about expansion, but equally encouraging is Ernest W. Brown, mayor and superintendent of the Metropolitan Police Department in Washington, D. C. "I consider the Woman's Bureau of this Department one of our most important units. As a matter of fact I have recommended an increase in the personnel of the woman's unit of this department."

Captain E. M. Slaughter of the Crime Prevention Division, Los Angeles Department of Police, said, "We find women police invaluable in cases involving women and children. There are numerous opportunities for the expansion of the women's program and no doubt it will come soon. The field of basic crime prevention...must be adequately covered if we are to stem the present tide of lawlessness, and there is much the policewoman can do in such a program."

You'd like to join the good fight, you say? Let us see just what the chances are of getting a police job in your town. If the appointments are not from a civil service list, you may need "political pull"—or a deceased husband who was a policeman. Although intelligence police officials or community pressure has often kept appointment standards high without civil service. If your community needs more policewomen, a little mobilization of public opinion may be in order. Perhaps the women's clubs can convince the mayor that more protective and preventive work is essential to his next election.

If, on the other hand, your city has civil service, find out when the next examinations are to be held, and "cram." Municipal laws, for one thing. Passing the exams creditably does not, of course, insure appointment. There aren't many being made these days, while the application list grows. "We find here in Washington a steadily increasing number of persons interested in entering our service, and for the recent civil service examination there was a surprisingly large group of women with excellent qualifications," said Miss Rhoda J. Milliken, director of the Woman's Bureau in the capital.

And while you wait you grow no younger. A policewoman's life used often, literally, to begin at forty. Maturity was supposed to be an asset. Now there is a distinct tendency to lower the age limits. Baltimore, Buffalo, Newark (New Jersey) enter women between 25 and 35 years; Los Angeles brings the lower limit down to 23, and New Orleans and San Francisco, while leaving the upper limits at 40 and 45 respectively, will consider applicants of 21. Detroit sets 25 to 30 years as the age for entering the service and in New York, where a woman is still eligible up to the age of 40, the mayor is urging that the limits be set at 21 to 29 years, the same as for men.

A few years ago the International Association of Policewomen (undone by the depression, unhappily), the United States Civil Service Commission, and the International Association of Chiefs of Police agreed upon a desirable minimum standard for women who enter police work. It is approximately a high school education plus two years in social work, preferably case work dealing with delinquents. (Now that social work is requiring college, the stipulations will need changing.) While political interference or ignorance of officials have lowered the standards in many instances, frequently cities have even higher requirements.

Thus in Detroit the minimum educational qualifications for appointment in the Women's Division are a college or university degree, one year in an approved school of social work, or special studies or achievements that "seem to warrant expectation of success and progress in the field of protective police work." There must have been a year's experience in a social organization of recognized standing, or two or more years in a closely related field.

Besides physical tests, Detroit gives a neurological examination and standard psychometric tests, to disclose, besides intelligence rating, such qualities as auditory and visual memory, powers of observation, and capacity for reasoning.

Most of the police executives writing Independent Woman stressed the need for "high moral character" in a policewoman. Certainly she must be tolerant and sympathetic in dealing with behavior problems of women and girls. She must, herself, be well adjusted to life, and have a good measure of emotional stability.

There is no knowing what exigency is just around the corner for a police worker, and many of her tasks are far from pleasant.

No schools offer special training for a policewoman, but obviously many of the courses in schools of social work and universities would be valuable to her. Nurse training and experience are regarded with an especially friendly eye. In New York and some other large cities the newly appointed women attend the three months' Police Academy along with the men. Where no such training is available, it is a matter of serving an apprenticeship—and the worker is on probation from three to six months, until she proves her mettle. Though not universally the case, more often than in other lines of work, policewomen receive the same pay as men, though only in a few cities do they have the same right of advancement and progressive increases. Washington, D. C., and Cleveland are among the latter, permitting advancement up to captaincies. Heretofore paid $200 a year less than men similarly classified, Detroit women will after July 1 be on the same basis: the initial $2,100 will be increased to $2,520 after a year, with $2,710 for sergeants. In New York men and women are paid alike, with $2,000 at the outset which increases each year until at the end of five years the salary is $3,000—subject to depression cuts. But patrolwomen, policewomen and investigators are all the same rank, except for Mrs. Mary A. Sullivan, director of the Bureau of Policewomen, whose salary is $4,000.

In smaller cities the figures are, of course, somewhat lower, but the pay is always comparable to that received by teachers and social workers. And there are the further benefits of pension possibilities and—if under civil service—security. Asked if many policewomen leave the service, one official snorted, "Leave? You couldn't pry them out of their jobs with a crowbar!"

Police work is not monotonous, certainly. Your "clients" run the whole gamut of social maladjustment. You are in court matching wits with magistrates and attorneys one day; the next perhaps, in disguise, having your fortune told by a gypsy who has been mulcting the gullible public. Besides its variety, the work offers a sense of getting at fundamentals, the satisfaction of human service.

On the other hand, in many police departments a woman—no matter what her capabilities—must still meet the prejudice engendered by political appointees without training or ambition. Furthermore, where there is no distinct woman's bureau the most able detective may be assigned to work under a precinct captain who, dead set against women around a station house, shunts her into some clerical job.

The policewoman's hours are sometimes long, and frequently odd. Though regular duties are usually done in 8-hour shifts, the investigator or detective must finish the problem in hand if it takes all night. And it requires sturdy character not to become depressed by constant contact with the maladjusted and depraved elements in the community.

But in her darkest hour, every policewoman can be sustained by knowledge that she is part of a worldwide movement. Even China now has its policewomen—in uniform, as are most of those in European countries. For some reason, possibly the earlier lifting of the depression abroad, women police are being decidedly increased in several places. After experimenting for a time with two, Paris has just appointed eighteen new women police assistants—thanks to pressure from the Conseil National des Femmes. In Spain, Barcelona had fourteen police women for patrol during the Exhibition in 1930, but after its close the group was disbanded. Now in revolutionary times women are again being appointed, one of their chief duties to be [to] search for illegal arms and ammunition. Women are engaged in large numbers, it seems, to smuggle arms, and the Spanish policeman is notoriously averse to laying hands on a woman.

Mary Sullivan, first woman homicide detective (1912) and director of the NYPD Bureau of Policewomen (1926). (Photographer unknown.)

In London, where Commandant Mary S. Allen heads the Women's Auxiliary Service, the Home Secretary has just authorized the gradual increase of the metropolitan women's force from fifty-three to 142, with more women to be used as detectives. English cities and boroughs outside London have seventy-six policewomen.

Sixteen other countries courteously responded to Independent Woman's request for up-to-date information. "The employment of women police has been entirely satisfactory and it is realized that they are a necessity," writes H. E. Jones, chief officer of the Commonwealth Police in Australia. All the states have a corps, a total of thirty-four policewomen for the continent. Poland, beginning in 1925, has developed in the different cities a force of 120 policewomen.

Progressive little Finland has had women police since 1907, but the depression has given many of their jobs to men. Toronto, Canada, has women police. Copenhagen has nine policewomen under a woman director, and other Danish cities have followed her example. In Holland nine towns have a total of twenty women inspectors and twenty-two constables, but ground has been lost during the depression. Switzerland has eight women in four cities. Kaunas, Lithuania, has two college graduates, the first appointed in 1934, who "have proved that they are able to clear up crimes as well as a man would do it." Argentina, Belgium, Greece, Roumania and New Zealand report no women in the service, except in some instances in office work. In Hungary one of the three women detectives appointed ten years ago is still in the service, but will be pensioned off soon—and no new appointments are contemplated.

The women of Istanbul, Ankara, Izmir, and Adana have changed their veils of only a decade ago for visored caps. Of them the Director General of Public Surety of the Turkish Republic writes, "All Turkish policewomen are performing their duties very efficiently and I am expecting to augment their numbers in the near future." And in Dublin, though the four women police attached to the Garda Siochana are "in a sense experimental," still they have proven, besides efficient in women's cases, "particularly useful in the detection of begging, fortune-telling, shebeening." (Bootlegging, we'd call that last.) The duties of foreign policewomen are, in broad outline, the same as in America, except that a greater proportion of their time is spent dealing with commercialized prostitution.

Germany made no reply to Independent Woman's query, but she was a leader in the policewoman movement. Stuttgart named the first policewoman in the entire world in 1903, and they used to be found in large numbers in all Germany's principal cities. Unverified reports say that all have now been dismissed.

A list compiled three years ago by *The Policewoman's Review*, published by the Women's Auxiliary Service in London (the only policewoman's publication, incidentally) adds to the countries noted having women police, Austria, Burma, Norway, Portugal, Sweden, Uruguay, Egypt, Mexico and, of course, Russia. "Policeman Lily travels fearlessly through dark woods about the city to round up criminal gangs. On one occasion, when she was conveying a prisoner caught setting fire to turf fields, she was set upon in the woods by two of his accomplices and brought back to jail not one criminal but three," reports Anna Louise Strong in the newly published *This Soviet World*.

Several women in the United States hold unique jobs in the police field. The Massachusetts State Police seems to be the only state unit employing policewomen. It has two. West Virginia has two county sheriffs who are women. They are Mrs. Pearl T. Hickman, sheriff of Monongalia

County, Morgantown, and Mrs. Effie Dwyer, sheriff of Cabell County, Huntington. Two of Nebraska's ex-sheriffs are women, and Miss Fern W. Ritner is now serving as deputy sheriff of Lincoln County at North Platte. There is, also, Captain Pearl L'Heureux (an important Kansas Federation member, incidentally) who heads, not a women's bureau, but a crime prevention bureau in Wichita. The Federal Government has no women as Department of Justice agents, nor as agents in the Secret Service, though women are employed as informers and detailed on special cases.

Witness, however, the appointment last summer of youthful Marie Grott as head of the criminal identification bureau of the Indiana State Police. The promotion was due to her excellent work in the Dillinger and other important criminal cases. ❧

In *Police Women: Life with the Badge*, authors Sandra Wells and Betty Sowers Alt conclude, "By the end of the Depression (in the early 1940s), there were only a thousand publicly funded police women hired by fewer than 3 percent of the nation's law enforcement agencies. The Depression decade had taken a toll on women' progress in policing."

Three women who rose as shining stars in the police work despite this national decline were Eleonore Hutzel in Detroit, Mary Shanley in New York, and Mabel Lena Cramer Kruse in Akron, Ohio.

Michigan Women's Hall of Fame
Eleonore Hutzel (1885–1979)
Inducted: 1999
Era: Historical
Areas of Achievement: Nursing, Social Work/Mission Work

Born September 8, 1885, in Ann Arbor, Michigan, Eleonore Hutzel came to Detroit in 1910 to study nursing at Harper Hospital while studying obstetrics at Woman's Hospital and working as a Visiting Nurse. Hutzel became interested in social service and after finishing her nurse's course, moved to Chicago where she attended and graduated from what later became the School of Social Services. She returned to Detroit in 1915 as the first director of social services for Woman's Hospital for unwed mothers and their children. Her interest in the poor and underprivileged led to membership on the board of the Girls' Protective League, which in turn, led to the organization of the first Women's Division of the Detroit Police Department.

In 1922 Hutzel was the first woman to head the Detroit Police Department's Women's Division. More importantly, she was instrumental in making "an experiment" her career. Shortly after assuming directorship of the Women's Division, the newly-appointed police commissioner, Frank Croul, made clear that he did not think such a division was necessary, but would give Hutzel six months to show its worth.

Six months later, Hutzel was appointed fourth deputy commissioner and chief of the Women's Division. Hutzel had never set foot in a police station before becoming the head of the Women's Division. The division was only one year old when she took over with a staff of sixteen officers and responsibility as a protective agency for all children up to ten and girls up to seventeen, as well as handling crimes involving women in the City of Detroit.

In 1939 Hutzel also was named trustee of Woman's Hospital. In 1964 the Woman's Hospital Board of Trustees, in recognition of her achievements in the social work and health/human services area, changed the name of the hospital to Hutzel Hospital in her honor.

Hutzel spent her life working in a field that demands strength, intelligence, and integrity. She was a pioneer in the advancement and acceptance of women within law enforcement, criminal justice, and social work, and she was equally devoted to all men, women, and children who were in need of help, guidance, and love.

Meet "Deadshot Mary," a 1930s Undercover Cop Superstar

By Hadley Meares

Atlas Obscura, May 25, 2016

How one NYC policewoman became a media sensation.

On June 20th, 1938, pedestrians near bustling Herald Square in Midtown Manhattan were treated to a scene right out of a dime store novel. A well-dressed middle-aged woman was fighting with a man, attempting to subdue him. He pushed her in the face, and she retaliated, knocking him into submission with a swing of her long strapped pocket book. The man was lucky she did not use the gun tucked carefully into the folds of her dress.

The man was a suspected jewel thief, and his captor was an undercover policewoman with the press sobriquet of "Deadshot" Mary. "Well, I got him," she told two patrolmen who had rushed to the scene to help, "and I can take him in myself."

Detective Mary Shanley of the New York Police Department, sometimes known as "Deadshot," 1937. (*Mary A. Shanley, New York City detective - "pickpockets' captor fears that she might look tough."* Photograph. Retrieved from the Library of Congress, <www.loc.gov/item/2004676753/>.)

"Deadshot" Mary Shanley was born in Ireland in 1896. Her family immigrated to America, and in 1931, the boisterous and brave Mary joined the NYPD. This was an unusual step for a woman of her time, though not unheard of.

During the first half of the 20th century, policewomen in America often worked undercover, on so-called "women's beats." "They are called upon regularly to trail or trap mashers, shoplifters, pickpockets and fortune-tellers; to impersonate drug addicts and hardened convicts, to expose criminal medical practice, find lost persons, guide girls in trouble, break up fake matrimonial bureaus and perform special detective duty," wrote the *New York Times*.

For most of her career, Mary would be assigned to the NYPD pickpocket squad. By the time of her retirement in 1957, she would be a first grade detective, with over 1,000 arrests under her belt.

Mary cut her teeth on the force working undercover to catch fortune-tellers who set up storefronts in buildings all across Manhattan. Fortune-telling was illegal at the time, partially because of prejudice against the immigrant communities where it was popular, and partly because it was seen as a swindle most likely to ensnare lonely, vulnerable, white women.

Undercover policewomen would visit the fortune-tellers, and after paying for their readings, arrest them. In 1931, the *New York Times* reported on Shanley's arrest of a certain ingenious soothsayer named Princess Juniata Flynn:

> *Policewoman Shanley...unwrapped a striped bandanna handkerchief from the head of the "Princess," revealing a telephone head set resting snugly against her ears. The basket into which written questions were put revealed a false bottom which led to an assistant who telephoned the inquiries to the seer, who would repeat the questions, amazing her clients.*

In December 1934, a change came to the NYPD. The 140 or so female police officers on the force were now required to carry guns (the practice had been voluntary before) when they prowled department stores, shopping centers, and crowded entertainment areas. They were issued 16-ounce revolvers, which were half the weight of the guns policemen carried, and were required to take target practice.

"On the practice range in headquarters' basement some of the women have proved more gun shy than others," a reporter patronizingly wrote. "But none has figured in an 'I didn't know it was loaded' mishap. Neither has any hit the bullseye ten times in a row for a perfect 100, though several have broken 80."

A few years later, Mary became the first policewoman in the history of the NYPD to use a gun during a capture and arrest, when she fired into the air while pursuing a racketeer on 53rd Street. Around this time, local papers began to report on her exploits, amazed that a five-foot-eight, 160-pound woman had the strength to subdue grown men, sometimes two at a time!

"Mary Shanley ordered two suspicious characters, neither of them weaklings, into the lobby of the Longacre Building in Times Square shortly after 10 o'clock last night," the *New York Times* reported breathlessly. "They complied, for everything in the policewoman's mien indicated determination—even the firm grasp of her right hand on her service pistol. Searching them in the lobby and finding on them...imitation pistols, she arrested them on charges of carrying concealed weapons."

These cameos in the crime blotters earned her the enduring nickname "Deadshot Mary," as well as comparisons to the legendary sharpshooter Annie Oakley. She became a media darling, sometimes posing for pictures where she looked like a respectable middle-class matron, except for the gun she was pointing directly at the camera. In the Sunday series "Heroines of Today," illustrator Nell Brinkley depicted an idealized Shanley shooting her gun, capturing criminals, and tucked into a stylish bed reading a mystery novel and eating crackers.

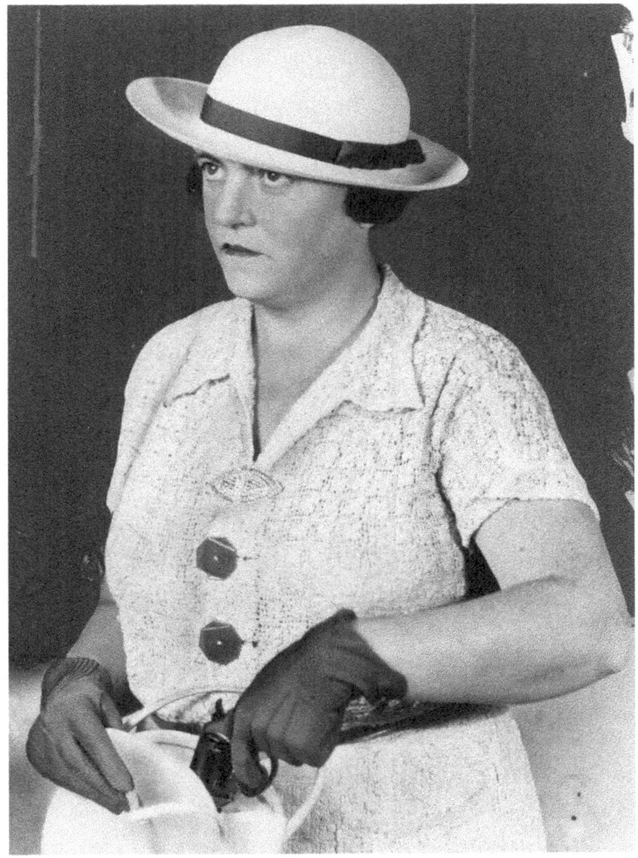

Shanley was the first policewoman in the NYPD to use a gun to capture a suspect. (*Mary Agnes Shanley, New York City detective, half-length portrait, facing left, pulling a pistol out of her handbag*. Photograph. Retrieved from the Library of Congress, <www.loc.gov/item/2004676751/>.)

Mary also gave many interviews. She told the *New York World Telegram* that she respected stick-up men, because "at least they pick out places that can afford to get robbed." Overall, she "never felt sorry" for any of the people she arrested. Speaking with the *Panama City Herald*, Mary described her typical day searching for crooks:

> *"Detectives assigned to the pickpocket squad aren't given leads," says Detective Shanley, who has red hair and hazel eyes and looks as though she might be a college physical education instructor, "so I start my day by dressing to suit the neighborhood I have decided to work in."*
>
> *All day long, she wanders through department stores, stands in theater lines, and pushes her way into crowds. Five times a day she reports to the department by telephone. When anyone*

looks suspicious, she follows him or her, as the case may be. Usually it's a her, for Detective Shanley does her work where there are crowds of women.

"I can usually tell in 20 minutes whether a suspect is legitimate or not. Often when I have a hunch there is something phony about a woman, I trail her a whole day without seeing her try anything funny. If that happens, I trail her home, and then look for her picture in the police files. If I find it, I keep after the woman until I catch her at work."

"She could smell them I tell you," niece Mary Shanley Mullins remembered in the 2006 documentary *Sleuthing Mary Shanley*. "Macy's loved her. That was a great spot for pickpockets." Sometimes, the policewoman would take her niece to work with her: "I would be a decoy for her. She didn't look like a detective looking for a pickpocket, she was a mother out with her daughter."

In August 1939, Shanley was promoted to the rank of first-grade detective, only the fourth woman in the history of the NYPD to receive this honor. The year before, the NYPD had offered the first civil service exam for aspiring policewomen. Some 3,700 women took the exam, and 20 were accepted into the Police Academy the next year. There can be little doubt that Mary's recorded feats encouraged some women to pursue law enforcement careers.

According to Mullins, Mary "was not interested in a husband. She enjoyed her life. She had her freedom and her good salary. She was just different. She was very outspoken, very opinionated. She didn't fit in then as well as she probably would now. She was born too soon."

Mary's status as a role model was briefly tested in 1941, when she was suspended for firing her NYPD-issued gun while drinking off-duty in a bar in Jackson Heights, Queens. Mary claimed she had been under a doctor's care after surgery for a job-related injury. She had felt dizzy, ordered a whisky to steady herself and blacked out. Whatever the truth of the story, she was quickly reinstated to her beat.

As Mary got older, she didn't lose her tough edge. In 1950, she was working at a Macy's store in Queens when a 22-year-old mentally ill man burst into the store brandishing a .32 caliber automatic pistol. As customers ducked for cover behind display counters, Mary quietly approached the man from behind, gun in hand, and snapped, "Drop that gun, boy." The gun fell to the floor and the man was arrested.

Three years later, she was casing St. Patrick's Cathedral, trailing a woman and man who were stealing pocketbooks at the church altar. When she attempted to arrest them, the woman began to pull and claw at Mary so her partner could get away. Mary fired warning shots to stop the man, terrifying shoppers on Fifth Avenue. This was a signature Mary move—firing her service weapon

Shanley receiving congratulations from New York Mayor Fiorello La Guardia, 1937. (*Mary A. Shanley being congratulated by Mayor La Guardia, Deputy Chief Inspector John Lyons looks on.* Photograph. Retrieved from the Library of Congress, <www.loc.gov/item/2004676752/>.)

into the air instead of maiming a fleeing person. (This was before firing into the air became illegal in most states.)

In 1955, a group of matinee theater goers were treated to a vintage Mary arrest. At a screening of a movie called *Vera Cruz* at the Capital Theater, an undercover Mary noticed a known seat-tipper (a thief who "sees a handbag on an empty seat, tips the seat from the rear with his foot and loots the bag") attempting to steal a woman's unattended purse. At first, the arrest proceeded smoothly:

> *The suspect accompanied Detective Shanley—she was in her Sunday best, with a pale blue hat and bright earrings lending a gay touch to her gray hair—to the rear of the orchestra. But before she could complete the arrest, the man punched her, broke away and headed down the center aisle. It was at this point that the shots from the Detective's service revolver slammed harmlessly into the floor. Meanwhile, the fugitive did not get far. A retired patrolman, John Duffy...sized up the situation. Dropping the role of spectator, Mr. Duffy grappled with the man and brought him down with no great difficulty.*

After a medical check, Mary brought the perp to the station to be booked. "It's exciting," Mary told a reporter in 1937, when asked about her career. "I'd die if I had to go back to working in an office."

Mary retired from the NYPD in 1957, after more than a quarter-century on the police force. She spent the rest of her life in the state where New York Mayor Fiorello La Guardia had singled her out for demonstrating "not only keen intelligence and fine police work but also courage at a moment when courage was needed."

Policewoman "Deadshot" Mary Shanley died at the age of 93, and is buried on Long Island.

Akron Policewoman Battled Vice and Crime in 1930s and 1940s

By Akron Beacon Journal Staff

Akron Beacon Journal, March 23, 2008

It was an unusual journey from PTA president to vice squad officer, but Kruse served both posts with distinction.

"Any public service job is simply the art of getting along with people," she once told the Beacon Journal. "And I enjoy it—always have."

Mabel Lena Cramer, the youngest of four children, was born Aug. 12, 1887, to Melancthon and Zadia Cramer in Ashtabula County. She grew up in East Plymouth, attended local schools and trained as a nurse at Lakeside Hospital in Cleveland.

In the early 20th century, her parents moved to a dairy farm off Wyoga Lake Road in Northampton Township.

Mabel met her future husband, Arthur Kruse (pronounced KRU-zee), at Springfield Lake Park where she sold tickets in the dance pavilion. He was a violinist and orchestra leader who performed at the resort for 15 summers.

After marrying in 1908, the couple settled on Parkwood Avenue in Akron and welcomed four children: Carl, Robert, Arthur and Irma.

While her husband taught music lessons, Mabel Kruse juggled domestic life with a busy schedule. She joined the Home and School League, served as president of the Henry School PTA and Chi Theta Tau Mothers' Club, and counseled parent-teacher groups in Akron.

She also was active in politics, serving as president of the Ohio Women's Republican Club.

Portrait of a young Mabel Kruse, who would not enter police work until she was fifty years old. (Courtesy Bobbi Harmon.)

When her husband took ill during the Great Depression, Mabel accepted a job in 1935 as assistant matron at the city workhouse, a facility that housed misdemeanor offenders. Kruse was a strong, stocky woman who stood about 5-foot-8. She was tough when necessary, but she earned respect through kindness and fairness.

In March 1937, Akron Mayor Lee D. Schroy appointed her to be the city's only policewoman. The rookie cop was 50 years old.

The gray-haired Kruse wore silver glasses, a dark dress and a stylish hat. She practiced marksmanship at the police range and kept her pistol in a handbag.

Her assignment was to "save girls from wayward paths." She patrolled seedy hangouts in an effort to deter juveniles from vice and crime.

"Mrs. Kruse visits places that many men wouldn't enter alone," Beacon Journal reporter Marjorie McNab wrote in a 1939 profile. "She enters questionable nightspots where three-fourths or more of the lounging characters have appeared in police court. She keeps a watchful eye on 'dine and dance' places in search of wrongdoing beneath an outward air of innocence."

The motherly figure searched for teens in honky-tonk bars with blaring music and cheap booze. McNab described one such bar where "frowsy women with unkempt hair" flirted with "sparse-haired men" in "frayed, wrinkled suits."

The officer recognized many of the customers as women who had appeared before the health board for cure of social diseases.

"So many of these people are here because of wrecked homes, and because their childhoods went unguarded by careless parents," Kruse said. "Most of the children I find in these places are here for the same reason. They're seeking diversion from constant unhappiness at home."

Kruse wanted to break the terrible cycle. She advocated a system where social workers checked up on prostitutes after their jail sentences ended.

"As it is now, many girls have no place to go after they get out, and just sink back into a life of crime again," she said.

The officer's job was to reach the "erring girls" before they toughened up and got used to life on the town. "We do all we can for them but after they're picked up a certain number of times, arrest doesn't mean much to them," she said.

After two years of riding in vice squad cars and doing general police work, Kruse had to defend her title. The city required her to take a civil service exam and fitness test in March 1939.

Kruse competed with police candidates Catherine McGee, Virginia Stoffer, Violet Cash Weisberg and Lillian Wargo. The women met at the YWCA gym to run laps, skip ropes, do push-ups, vault a pommel horse and toss a 50-pound sandbag to prove that they could "cope with mashers."

Names of the top three were forwarded to Mayor Schroy.

Officer Kruse easily retained her job, the first Akron policewoman hired under civil service.

The force added five women in the next decade. Kruse was featured with two other officers—Jo Bowland and Jessie Melnik—in a 1946 pictorial that appeared in the Beacon Journal.

The women demonstrated a "lost pocketbook swindle" as a warning to readers. Bowland and Melnik portrayed con artists who conspired to bilk Kruse out of bank money after pretending to find a purse stuffed with cash.

In real life, Kruse was no dupe.

She handled court cases for five years, appearing with female defendants. She ducked a few punches in her time, but she never had to use her gun on duty.

One day, a woman tried to run away from Akron Municipal Court. Too bad for her.

There were no escapes on Kruse's watch.

"I had to grab her hair and hold," she later recalled. "Nearly pulled it out."

Mabel and her husband moved from Akron to the Wyoga Lake farm that her parents had owned. Arthur Kruse's health continued to deteriorate. He died of stomach cancer in 1947.

Kruse became the first policewoman in Akron, Ohio. (Courtesy Bobbi Harmon.)

In 1948, Mabel Kruse partnered with Officer Lillian Kirkpatrick, a WAC during World War II. The white-haired Kruse and dark-haired Kirkpatrick stood out on patrol. "Officer Lil" learned the beat from Kruse and remained with the department for 26 years.

Kruse finished her career with the detective bureau, retiring in 1952 when she turned 65.

"I thought it was time to quit," she explained. "I've got a big family, lots of things to do. I'll get down to the station occasionally, though—you couldn't keep me away."

Mabel Kruse was 85 when she died July 7, 1973. She was buried next to her husband in Oakwood Cemetery in Cuyahoga Falls.

Akron native Bobbi Harmon, 66, of Tucson, Ariz., recalls her grandmother as a feisty woman with a great sense of humor.

"She was a character," Harmon said. "I loved her dearly."

Kruse was proud of her police career and liked to regale her wide-eyed granddaughter with gritty tales from the vice squad—sometimes to the chagrin of Harmon's mother.

Harmon still recalls some of those anecdotes.

"None that you can print," she said with a laugh. ❧

Although the Depression of the 1930s led to a decline in hiring in all but a few cities, the wartime of the next decade would lead to a surge. The progressive work that women had been building in police forces was not so easily regained, however.

Chapter 5
World War II

The World War II era is often referred to as a time of great growth for women in the workforce. Thousands of American men were fighting overseas, and women were called upon to do to their duty in the factories and beyond. It was the era of Rosie the Riveter, and America celebrated tough, resourceful women. Looking back, it would be reasonable to infer that policewomen thrived during this time, taking up more patrol work and claiming equal footing with men on police forces. But the opposite was true, unfortunately.

A History of Women in Policing
National Center for Women & Policing, 2013

World War II brought changes to policing personnel. More women were hired during the war, but most of these women were confined to auxiliary work. The women that joined the police force during this period were there to assist new men employed, who could not join the military, in their duties. So women worked as dispatchers or clerical workers within the departments, whereas men still had patrol duties and worked as the crime fighters. Women worked primarily as either helpers to the men or they worked with children and young women. The role that women police officers originally filled as social workers still strongly defined how women were used in the police force. ❧

The pre-Depression preventive and protective work that policewomen had championed had still not returned, and as child delinquency shot up during World War II, policewomen were restless for meaningful change. While this was visible across the country, Detroit made headlines, primarily because its women's division was headed up by Eleonore Hutzel, who adamantly implemented the same preventive and protective tactics that had proved successful before the Great Depression.

Women training with the Los Angeles Police Department, 1948. Left to right, Melva Myers, Betty Webster, Norma Johnston, Janet Elvedahl, and Betty Hern. (uclalat_1429_b41_52093-1, *Los Angeles Times* Photographic Archives [Collection 1429]. Library Special Collections, Charles E. Young Research Library, UCLA.)

Job for a Lady

By Vera Connolly

Collier's Weekly, June 10, 1944

Detroit's women police tackle the girl-delinquency problem with a common-sense, humane plan that gets results—and provides a sound working model for other cities

It was a stormy night last month. At midnight a gusty wind was blowing sheets of rain down the dark Detroit streets. But the policewoman in whose car I sat continued tirelessly to search a sordid neighborhood of cheap restaurants, all-night theaters and dingy rooming houses for a missing girl.

The child was Betty-May, a twelve-year-old runaway from Cleveland. At eight o'clock, word had been flashed to the women's division of the Detroit Police Department that the girl had headed for Detroit. And Miss Kidder, crack policewoman just setting out on her night patrol, had added this urgent search to her other duties.

I had been permitted to accompany her, for I was in Detroit to watch this celebrated group of fifty-eight women, headed by Eleonore L. Hutzel, at work. These women are doing a superb job in girl protection—at a time when in most cities girl delinquency is skyrocketing. National figures just released by the F.B.I. show that arrests of girls under twenty-one, in 1943, jumped 130.4 per cent over those in 1941.

After midnight we began dropping into gaudy, dim-lit taxi-dance halls to make sure no hostesses under twenty-one were employed. We visited all-night movie theaters in search of sleeping runaways, found two girls of eleven and twelve, drove them to their homes and rebuked their maddening, casual parents. (All law-enforcement officers are grimly bitter on the subject, urging that delinquent parents be brought to justice.)

Miss Kidder and I searched noisy beer gardens, blue with smoke, for girls under twenty-one. We inspected hot-dog joints, night clubs, skating rinks, public dance halls, cheap rooming houses and other spots likely to attract bewildered runaways, V-girls, and restless young thrill seekers.

"I think we'll drop into the bus terminal," Miss Kidder said suddenly. "Sometimes runaways sleep there."

And there, sure enough, sound asleep on a bench, her small cardboard suitcase on her lap, her feet drawn up under her, was a pretty blond child of twelve in plaid coat and cap. It was Betty-May;

though when first awakened, she assured us she was Miss Deanna Garbo of Denver. She slept soundly in the back of our big limousine all the way to the Juvenile Detention Home. In her purse was thirty cents. Not enough for a night's lodging. What would become of Betty-May the following night?

"She'll be sent home?" I asked, as we swung back to our last three hours of night patrol.

"Probably. If the home is possible at all, it's always the best place for a child. But we don't send a runaway back to drunkenness or cruelty; or to a brother or father who raped her. Each case is investigated thoroughly."

I thought of some other cities where treatment of girl runaways is still archaic, brutal and stupid. No investigations are made. Nondelinquent runaways are returned to homes often degrading and unbearable—from which they will run away again. Delinquent runaways are publicly arrested, thrown into reeking county jails with hardened criminals, tried, sent to a House of Correction for sixty days and then turned loose in a strange city without money, a job, or any assistance in going straight—without even shelter for one night.

City clocks were striking one-thirty as we began to patrol our tough, dim-lit district. The rain had stopped. Shadowy figures, on the arms of soldiers and sailors, were emerging from the dance halls, bars and cheap movie houses.

"Aren't these young girls?" I asked.

"Oh no," Miss Kidder said. "At a distance you can tell age by the legs; close up, by the hands. These are women twenty-five or more. But look! Over there. See that girl coming out of Tony's Restaurant with a civilian? She's young. We'll question her."

The Kindly Hands of the Law

She ran the car to the sidewalk, and we jumped out. She [approached] the couple, showed her badge and explained that this was not an arrest, just questioning. She took the girl quietly by the wrist. Instantly the man, who was about thirty-five, turned and fled. The thin, white-faced girl looked after him in fright. She was a nice youngster, rather shy, with clear skin, blue eyes and curling dark hair tied at the temple with a gay red bow. She wore only a thin silk coat, no hat. She was shivering.

"How old are you?" Miss Kidder asked.

"Twenty-three."

"It's better to tell the truth."

"I'm seventeen."

"Your name?"

She gave it. (We will call her Jean.)

"Does your mother know you're out this late?"

"I'm from Akron. I came to Detroit to live with my aunt."

"We'll take you home to your aunt."

"Oh, no. She's left Detroit."

"I see. Hop in. We'll go to police headquarters."

Miss Kidder's kind, expert questioning brought out the whole story. Jean had run away from a drunken father and a stepmother in Akron, selling her cloth coat to get train fare. She had come to Detroit to live with an aunt while studying stage dancing. The aunt, she found, had moved away.

Claiming to be twenty-one and experienced, Jean had taken a job as a dancer in the chorus of a cheap vaudeville theater. Unfamiliar with dance routines, she had not made good and had finally been fired. She had been unable to get another job. The evening before we found her, her landlady had put her out. Hungry and chilled, she had begged her way into an all-night movie house and gone to sleep. Later a man sitting next to her had seen her crying and had offered to buy her a meal. He had taken her to Tony's Restaurant.

"Where was he taking you when we picked you up?"

"He was going to rent a room for me."

"You mean—for both of you?"

"No. He said not. He promised..."

Miss Kidder turned directly to the girl.

"Jean, have you had anything to do with men or boys, sexually? If you have, you should be examined for venereal disease."

"No," was the vehement protest. "I never have. Never! But go ahead, examine me. I don't mind."

"Good. Now, Jean, we'll have to detain you here at headquarters while your case is investigated. You'll be in a clean, private room. Not with anyone else. And you are *not* being arrested or given a police record. You are just being protected."

"Don't send me home!" the girl begged.

"Your home will be investigated. If it's what you claim it is, you won't have to go back. If you do stay in Detroit, we'll help you get adjusted. Social agencies will find you a clean place to live, a job, some young friends and some fun. You'd like that?"

Tears of relief sprang to the girl's eyes. "Yes," she said huskily.

Jean's case illustrates girl-delinquency prevention at its best. It represents all-out community effort based on a simple program. Any city can set it up. Some cities are doing so through the following five preliminary steps.

1. Create in the police department a crime-prevention bureau. Within it, set up a women's division staffed with experts scientifically trained to discover girls in moral peril; interview them; transport them to their homes or to clean, proper detention places; thoroughly investigate them and refer the cases for solution to the right public and private agencies.
2. Provide the clean, proper detention places mentioned above.
3. Provide a Children's Court or the equivalent, with competent probation officers. Insist that judge and probation officers be Civil Service, and not political appointees.
4. Finance public and private agencies so that they can give delinquents and potential delinquents the careful, long-term aid many of the cases require. (Some cities are not only rehabilitating delinquent girls and boys but are beginning to clean up the areas that produced them.)
5. Punish parents guilty of willful neglect.

Any city should find this delinquency-prevention program fairly simple. It demands no lavish expenditure. The machinery for much of it is already in existence. It will greatly reduce local costs of crime and venereal-disease control. (Syphilis among 15- to 19-year-olds in New York rose 132% in 1943.) But most important of all—it will keep thousands of decent but neglected, restless girls from slipping into prostitution.

A policewomen's division need not be large. In Detroit, there are over 3,600 policemen, only 58 policewomen. In setting up a women's division, all authorities warn, the first essential is to staff it with specialists—keen and highly educated women thoroughly trained in psychology, sociology and law enforcement, and with practical experience in work with present-day youth. Some cities, proud of their up-to-the-minute policemen, appoint to the women's division the well-meaning but untrained, bungling widows of oldtime cops. Such officers evoke derisive laughter from modern delinquents, who can think in circles around them.

In the Detroit women's division—which is generally regarded as a model for the country—all entrants must possess a college degree or the equivalent, plus two years of practical experience in

Women applicants for the Los Angeles Police Department during their physical fitness test, circa 1940. (uclalat_1387_b33_23961-3, *Los Angeles Times* Photographic Archives [Collection 1429]. Library Special Collections, Charles E. Young Research Library, UCLA.)

work with youth. They must be between twenty-two and thirty, mentally alert, athletic, with great physical endurance and no serious physical defects.

After admission, the training is grueling. It includes not only the basic police curriculum, but very special training in work with youth, broad courses in psychology, sociology, penology and specific instruction in local law enforcement and crime prevention. These policewomen, when trained, can and do handle every known offense from simple loitering to the most vicious crimes in the calendar. In its twenty-three years of existence, the women's division has won the respect of the men in the department and the people of Detroit.

These women are quiet, refined and feminine. Some are extremely pretty. They have low voices. They dress in plain clothes and drive cars that bear no insignia. (This is to spare minors the shock and disgrace of public arrest, and to prevent life-long bitterness toward the law.) Yet all of these officers have an indescribable air of authority and power. They demand obedience and get it. All of them can shoot, if need be.

> Miss Hutzel, who heads this women's group, is one of the country's leading authorities on police procedure and is the author of a widely used police manual. I asked her how a small city, with limited funds for training women police, could hope to attract the right applicants and train them. She told me of a plan now under way and swiftly gathering momentum. The same project had been mentioned to me several weeks before in Washington, D. C., by Eliot Ness, director of the Office of Community War Services of the Federal Security Agency, and Mr. Charles J. Hahn, Jr., executive secretary of the National Sheriffs' Association.
>
> The idea is to establish a national school at which men and women police officers assigned to youth work, and coming to the school from all over the land, can be trained in modern scientific methods. The International Association of Chiefs of Police is determinedly behind this and is endeavoring to get it publicly or privately financed and launched at some university....
>
> We've always had some girl delinquents; probably always will. But this flock of excited little moths flying from neglect at home to the bright lights of the cities, getting singed and disappearing down dark streets—this is a grim product of the war. Almost the only hope of rescue lies in discovery by the police—especially by some alert, diligent policewoman scientifically trained for this work....
>
> If this country had a smallpox epidemic, we'd stop it—and immediately. This epidemic of juvenile delinquency is no less grave! ❧

As World War II was coming to a close, Imra Buwalda—whom we saw as one of the authors of *The Woman Citizen* series in the 1920s—felt it necessary to take a look at the policewomen movement's start, progression, roadblocks, and recent decline. She published an article titled "The Policewoman Yesterday, Today and Tomorrow" in the *Journal of Social Hygiene* in May 1945 to broadcast the current need for more policewomen. Crimes by girls and women were up by 44.6 percent according to the FBI, and Buwalda added that authorities were forecasting "a crime wave of unprecedented proportions." She teamed up with Captain Rhoda Milliken, chief of the Woman's Bureau of the Washington, D.C., Metropolitan Police Department, to analyze the nation's trends and figure just how many more policewomen were needed to promote safety and crime prevention: a colossal 3,000.

Buwalda closed her argument with: "It would be difficult...to overstate the importance and urgency of the appointment of qualified policewomen in the majority of American communities; in rendering them effective training aids and opportunities; and in awakening and keeping alive a far-reaching public understanding and support."

Newly appointed LAPD Police Commissioner Mrs. Curtis Albro, right, inspecting a new class of policewomen. Audrey Melane throws Sergeant George Danbacher, instructor, 1946. (uclalat_1429_b3_43080, *Los Angeles Times* Photographic Archives [Collection 1429]. Library Special Collections, Charles E. Young Research Library, UCLA.)

While Buwalda made a clear case for more policewomen, the following article argued that plenty of policewomen had been hired but were not trained well. Still, controversy swirled around women on police forces.

Expanding Role of Women in Police Service

Journal of Criminal Law, January–February 1946

An important contribution to the literature in the field of crime prevention has just been released jointly by the Federal Security Agency, the International Association of Chiefs of Police and the National Sheriffs' Association in the form of a 92 page manual, entitled *Techniques of Law Enforcement in the Use of Policewomen with Special References to Social Protection*. The manual was designed for the use of policewomen in the performance of their preventive-protective functions, and for the assistance of law enforcement administrators in the selection, assignment and most effective use of women public officers. It was compiled by the National Advisory Police Committee on Social Protection of the Federal Security Agency, embracing representatives from the organizations named above.

In two previous manuals approved by the National Advisory Police Committee, *Techniques of Law Enforcement Against Prostitution*, and *Techniques of Law Enforcement in the Treatment of Juveniles and the Prevention of Juvenile Delinquency*, emphasis was placed on the value of trained policewomen in both fields. During the war period many police departments added policewomen to their staffs, and there is a great demand for more. Few trained women are available to meet this demand. As a result it has been necessary to recruit untrained and inexperienced policewomen in many communities. Unfortunately schools for training new recruits are so few and so scattered that it is impossible for them to meet increasing current needs.

There is reason to believe that there will be an increase rather than a decrease in law enforcement problems during the difficult years of postwar readjustment, and hence the need for effective crime prevention programs on the part of the police will be greater than ever. In the last analysis, crime prevention is a community responsibility. No community plan to prevent crime and delinquency can be truly effective that overlooks the role of the law enforcement juvenile officer.

The primary purpose of this manual is to serve as an in-service training text in helping the newly appointed policewoman to learn her job; to give her practical suggestions for dealing with the child, the girl or the woman who is in difficulty either as an offender or as a victim of an offense; to show how she can most effectively participate in police and community programs to prevent delinquency and crime; and to stimulate her to undertake further self-education through reading and study suggested in the bibliography. It is also hoped that this manual may be useful to law enforcement executives in bringing to their attention the potential services of policewomen in helping to solve these urgent local problems. Copies of this publication may now be obtained free of charge by addressing Mr. Thomas Devine, Director, Social Protection Division, Community War Services, Federal Security Agency, Washington, D. C. —EDITOR ❧

The events of the Great Depression and the following war years drained the enthusiasm from the policewomen movement. Many young women came of age during these years and might have become policewomen, but for the most part they did not. Notable exceptions include Eleonore Hutzel, Mary

Shanley, Mabel Lena Cramer Kruse, and Rhoda Milliken, and we have them to thank for the survival of the policewomen movement. Despite challenges, women's police forces continued on into the second half of the twentieth century, when they would be bolstered by another wave of feminism but still have many obstacles to navigate.

Chapter 6
The Beginning of the Modern Era

The end of the Second World War worked a decisive change in the status of women, as it did all other aspects of American society. The most obvious change was the great increase in the status of women employed outside the home. The war opened up many new avenues of employment, especially in industry, that had hitherto been largely reserved for men. With the position of wage earner came new responsibilities as well as a new freedom. Shortly after came female sociologists, psychologists, economists, and others who began to examine the new roles played by women in the American society.

In 1956 the International Policewomen's Association was reinstated as the International Association of Police Women, having the same goals as before it was closed during the Depression but now on a broader scale. More policewomen were hired nationwide, and they fought for equal status with policemen, both in terms of hiring opportunities and to assume duties beyond what policewomen had been historically assigned. In 1969 the organization would implement a slight change of name: the International Association of Women Police (IAWP), which it holds to this day.

A History of Women in Policing

National Center for Women & Policing, 2013

The 1950s saw a doubling of the number of women in law enforcement in the United States. Although the overall number of women making up law enforcement officers remained relatively low, the 1950s saw a marked increase in the number of women officers. Perhaps even more encouraging, the 1950s and early 1960s for some women brought about a change in how women police officers saw their advancement in the profession. There was a new push to advance women in the profession through integration with the men. Some of the younger working-class women wanted to work in the same departments with men, doing the same work. This time period saw the re-establishment of the International Association of Women Police and an increased enthusiasm for the profession as

Policewomen at a shooting range in Los Angeles, 1948. (uclalat_1387_b114_41323-1, *Los Angeles Times* Photographic Archives [Collection 1429]. Library Special Collections, Charles E. Young Research Library, UCLA.)

a career distinct from that of social worker. All these changes led to greater demands for equal treatment and [opportunities] for women police officers, and in 1968 two women from the Indianapolis Police department were allowed to go on patrol duty just as the men got to. This was the beginning of a change in policing that would have a dramatic effect on women in law enforcement everywhere. The women's movement as well as advances in the law helped to change how women were able to excel on the police force throughout the 70's and 80's. In 1972 Title VII of the 1964 Civil Rights Act was expanded to include public agencies and as a result police departments were prohibited by law from discriminating against women in hiring, recruiting, promotions, and working conditions. Also at this time two laws, the Revenue Sharing Act and the Crime Control Act, both concentrated on withholding funds from departments that discriminated. From 1960 to 1980 the percentage of women in police agencies doubled and the greater numbers brought greater opportunities and challenges. From the 70's into the 90's women in law enforcement agencies have worked for an equal role in all facets of policing, on patrol, in command positions, and in promoting and recruiting officers. In 1985 Penny Harrington became the first woman to be named Chief of Police for a major city, Portland, Oregon, and in Atlanta, Georgia, in 1994 Beverly J. Harvard became the first African American woman to be made Chief of Police for a large city. These accomplishments are a strong testament to the courage and perseverance that women have shown throughout the history of women in policing. ❧

While women wanted their place in the workforce, there was also much concern about how they would fulfill their roles as wives and mothers as well. Florence R. Kluckhohn, a Harvard anthropology professor, assessed this new position.

American Women and American Values

By Florence R. Kluckhohn

The Annals of America 1950–1960, 1968

Even though I cannot agree with those who blame women so much, I concur in the opinion that a majority of women now find, and will continue to find it difficult to be both wives and mothers and also successful competitors in the occupations. Why then, if it is so difficult, are so many women already attempting to do both, others expressing the wish that they could, and still others showing signs of frustrations because they do not or cannot?

Kluckhohn argued that women should be accepted into the workforce but also suggested a custom arrangement to make it easier for them:

Women should…be trained for and allowed to have their regular place in the occupations, but preferably it should be the kind of job, or career, which is limited in time and scope.… Especially during the years of motherhood, the limited job seems much the better solution. ❧

South Pasadena's first female police officer, Shirley Largent, issuing parking ticket, 1963. (uclalat_1429_b518_222303, *Los Angeles Times* Photographic Archives [Collection 1429]. Library Special Collections, Charles E. Young Research Library, UCLA.)

While society may have been pushing women to return to the home, or at least work "limited jobs" during this era, policewomen wanted full police duties just as much as ever and began to fight for appropriate leadership roles on the force. In 1956 the movement got the push it needed when the International Association of Police Women (later the IAWP) was reinstated.

The IAWP Past & Present

International Association of Women Police, 2017

In 1956, at a meeting of the Women Peace Officers of California, in San Diego, California, the Association was reorganized and recognized as the International Association of Police Women. Several years later the organization changed its name to the International Association of Women Police (IAWP). Under the direction of Doctor Lois Higgins, its newly elected President, IAWP began to change and grow. Dr. Higgins, a thirty-year member of the Chicago Police Department, held the position of IAWP President for eight years and then served twelve more years as its Executive Director.

Speaking at the first biannual meeting of the IAWP held at Purdue University in 1957, Dr. Higgins commented, "The advent of women into [police] departments brought into existence the crime prevention and juvenile bureaus.... These women brought a social viewpoint into police work."

The IAWP, through its constitution and activities, promoted separate women's bureaus. Many women felt this was their only opportunity for advancement within the department. Before 1969, women were never assigned to patrol, and many did not even own a uniform. Their duties were still restricted to those performed in the early 1900's by Mrs. Wells.

Though IAWP membership remained small through the 1960's, the IAWP began to hold annual three-day conferences in 1963. Attendance at the conferences was minimal. ❧

Police History: The Evolution of Women in American Law Enforcement

By Betsy Brantner Smith

PoliceOne, June 30, 2015

...The tide began to turn in the 1950s as women in law enforcement moved into more male-dominated roles and began to compete for promotion. In 1956 the International Association of Women Police

Elizabeth Coffal Robinson, at wheel, and Betty Blankenship, looking in window, one of the nation's first female patrol officer teams, of the Indianapolis Metropolitan Police. (Courtesy Lichtenberger History Room, Indianapolis Metropolitan Police Department.)

was formed, further supporting advancement for female officers. In the 1960s, as police departments increasingly battled prostitution and illegal drug sales, agencies developed an expanded need for women crimefighters to serve undercover in vice squads.

Finally, a major turning point occurred in 1968 when the Indianapolis Metropolitan Police Department assigned responsibility for Car 47 to the nation's first female patrol officers, Elizabeth [Coffal] Robinson and Betty Blankenship.... ❧

Legal advances for policewomen were in the works too. As Adam Eisenberg, author of *A Different Shade of Blue,* wrote:

Stella H. Bogan, one of three women taking the oath at a "unisex" training program at the Los Angeles Police Academy, 1973. (uclalat_1429_b723_276105, *Los Angeles Times* Photographic Archives [Collection 1429]. Library Special Collections, Charles E. Young Research Library, UCLA.)

In the early 1960s female officers in New York City sued for the right to take promotional exams alongside the men. When they won, policewomen across the nation were affected. By the turn of the decade, segregation had ended and policewomen were assigned to units department-wide, and by the early 1970s they were finally allowed to compete head-to-head with men on tests for sergeant. ❧

This came at a time when there was much unrest in America with the civil rights movement and protests against America's involvement in the Vietnam War, and the police image was faltering in the American view.

Public and Community Relations

By O. W. Wilson and Roy Clinton McLaren

Police Administration, 1977

The decade of the 1960s was marked by widespread riots, civil disorder, violent protests, increasing street crime, an explosion in the use of narcotics, assassination of public officials and national figures, and other manifestations of troubled society. Although the unrest centered in densely populated urban areas and on college campuses, few areas of the nation escaped its effects. The police were suddenly forced to consider the subject of "public relations" or "community relations" in a new way. As a result of the agonizing experience of these years, some fundamental concepts must now be recognized.

Policies Affecting Public and Community Relations

The emphasis in this field has shifted from a concentration on building the public image toward achievement of a comprehensive set of objectives and policies:

- Public support is essential to effective police administration.
- The motivation for increasing public support should be not so much to receive praise and support and support per se as to secure the benefit of the support in terms of increased finances and backing to do a better job.
- The only long-term way to improve the image of the police is to provide effective, enthusiastic, fair, and just service in as professional a manner as possible. Communicating the news of progress in this direction, however, should be deliberate and immediate.
- The police must realize that improvement in police services and the police image can be neither achieved overnight nor enhanced by adoption of superficial community relations programs. If the public senses that community relations programs are insincere, the efforts will probably fail.
- Improvement of police services can be facilitated through dialogue with the community.
- The community relations effort should emphasize crime resistance and public education programs.
- Fair and just treatment of all citizens should be a fundamental policy of the department.

In response, the Police Foundation was formed.

History of the Police Foundation

Police Foundation, 2016

Los Angeles Police officer Carolyn L. Wallace being awarded the Medal of Valor, 1972. (uclalat_1429_b704_272729, *Los Angeles Times* Photographic Archives [Collection 1429]. Library Special Collections, Charles E. Young Research Library, UCLA.)

The mission of the Police Foundation is to advance policing through innovation and science. It was established in 1970 by a grant from the Ford Foundation, and its work over almost five decades has proven to be a catalyst for significant changes in policing over the years. The Foundation relies on scientific evidence to address some of the most rudimentary and complex issues in the criminal justice system and on innovation to develop effective solutions rooted in its research or that of others. The Police Foundation's work over the years has enlightened scholars and practitioners alike, serving both as a model for systematic examination of real-world challenges and a stimulus for dialogue among the police, policy makers, scholars, the public, and the media. In large part, that ongoing dialogue has been responsible for the generation of new ideas for research and practice. The Police Foundation is non-profit, non-partisan, and independent, and it is not a membership organization.

The Police Foundation has ignited a spirit of collaboration among police, academic scholars, and community members. It has relied on its lasting and constructive relationships with police leaders, scholars, and government officials, as well as community groups and national organizations, in order to raise awareness of the complex challenges faced by law enforcement and the criminal justice system. Among these are the ability to balance the need for democratic policing consistent with constitutional mandates and civil liberties, with the need for enforcing laws, investigating crimes, and rendering justice. These challenges are among those of greatest importance to the Police Foundation.

Indeed, the Police Foundation is often engaged in controversial situations because it is committed to objective analysis, not partisan imperatives or special interests. We draw upon the latest advances in science and technology to challenge assumptions and seek solutions. We have always and will continue to address civil unrest and disturbances, as we were established in an era marked by significant civil unrest. We have also examined police ethics, abuse of authority, and use of force, as well as immigration enforcement and gun policy. But we also address the needs of police, from advancing the professionalization of police, including such issues as higher education and women in policing, to officer safety and well-being. In addition, we help develop the capacity of the police through training, education, and dissemination of the most promising or proven strategies for enhancing their effectiveness and efficiency, while maintaining public trust, safety, and security.

The Police Foundation has worked with police departments of all sizes, in every region of the United States and throughout the world. Our work is grounded in the practical world of policing; in advancing the science of policing and new ideas, strategies, and technologies to improve the quality of police services; and in maximizing public trust, accountability, and police legitimacy.

The Years Prior to the Police Foundation's Establishment

When the Police Foundation was created in 1970, the United States had recently experienced the devastation of riots in most of its large cities and many smaller ones. These riots were often allegedly sparked by discrimination, segregation, poverty, and police brutality in places like Los Angeles (Watts, 1965), New York (Harlem and Rochester in 1964, Stonewall in 1969), Philadelphia (1964), Detroit (1967), Omaha (1966), Chicago (1968), Newark (1967) and Minneapolis (1967), to name a few. In 1967 alone, there were over 150 race riots (known as the "long hot summer"). While few blamed the police for the societal conditions that led to the riots, every major riot was triggered by police actions in minority communities. The assassinations of both Malcolm X and Dr. Martin Luther King, Jr. further escalated racial tensions and civil unrest. Other factors, such as the passage in 1964 of Proposition 14 by California voters, effectively allowing homeowners to discriminate against prospective minority tenants or purchasers, may also have inflamed and increased tensions between government and citizens in places like Los Angeles. The decade was ushered in with sit-ins and the freedom rides in the South, and later in the decade, there were violent clashes during the Democratic National Convention in Chicago. Throughout the decade and across the country, there were increasing protests over the Vietnam War and its escalation. These began in cities and towns, as well as on college campuses across America.

While the civil disturbances of the 1960s were likely fueled by a variety of social conditions affecting marginalized communities, in many instances they were also motivated by police actions that many felt were unjust. At the same time, the 1960s had also seen escalating crime rates that even the most efficient police departments seemed powerless to reverse. Random patrol, reduced response time, and tactical police strategies—the trinity of the professional law enforcement model—seemed useless against a rising tide of crime, much of it driven by illegal drug marketing. In 1965, U.S. President Lyndon B. Johnson issued Executive Order 11236, which established "The President's Commission on Law Enforcement and the Administration of Justice." The Executive Order charged the Commission with the following tasks:

1. Inquire into the causes of crime and delinquency, measures for their prevention, the adequacy of law enforcement and administration of justice, and the factors encouraging respect or disrespect for law, at the national, State, and local levels, and make such studies, conduct such hearings, and request such information as it deems appropriate for this purpose.
2. Develop standards and make recommendations for actions which can be taken by the Federal, State, and local governments, and by private persons and organizations, to prevent, reduce, and control crime and increase respect for law, including, but not limited to, improvements in training and qualifications of personnel engaged in law enforcement and related activities, improvements in techniques, organization, and administration of law enforcement activities, improvements in the administration of justice, improvements in correction and rehabilitation of convicted offenders and juvenile delinquents, promotion of better understanding between law, enforcement officials and other members of the community, and promotion of greater respect for law throughout the community.

Nearly two years later, the 19 members of the Commission, 63 staff, 175 consultants and hundreds of advisors released their report, *The Challenge of Crime in a Free Society*, which contained more than 200 recommendations that the Commission "believes can lead to a safer and more just society," including a more robust level of support from the federal government, particularly the Department of Justice, in supporting the major burden that state and local governments are expected to carry in administering the criminal justice system of America.

Despite these important efforts, protests continued into the 1970s, perhaps peaking on May 4, 1970, when National Guard troops that had been called in by the governor of Ohio to quell anti-war protests on campus, shot at and killed four students at Kent State and injured even more. All of these issues raised questions about the role of police in managing civil disorder and maintaining order while balancing the rights of citizens, both at the individual and collective levels. The issues of civil unrest and disorder have re-emerged over time, leading to engagement by the Police Foundation in resolving and preventing such conflicts; a commitment that continues today. ❧

Ellen Cardiff, a retired sheriff's sergeant, being sworn in here by Judge Andrew Hauk as the nation's first woman U.S. marshal, 1971. (uclalat_1429_b680_268377, *Los Angeles Times* Photographic Archives [Collection 1429]. Library Special Collections, Charles E. Young Research Library, UCLA.)

Police History: The Evolution of Women in American Law Enforcement

By Betsy Brantner Smith

PoliceOne, June 30, 2015

...During the 1970s the presence of female officers in police departments became increasingly accepted by the general public, as is evidenced by the popularity of TV programs such as Policewoman and Get Christie Love. In 1972, Title VII of the Civil Rights Act was implemented outlawing gender discrimination in public agencies—including police departments—and further expanding opportunities for women in law enforcement. In July of that year JoAnne Misko and Susan Malone became the first fully sworn FBI agents in the U.S. Finally, the women's movement in this country generally made female service in formerly male-dominated roles increasingly acceptable, and law enforcement was no exception to this trend. ❧

Through the 1980s and 1990s, the same trends continued—more policewomen were hired and trained, and we saw them take on increased responsibilities, appearing more and more often on patrol and crime-fighting forces. Unfortunately, the issue of women not being treated entirely equally in police forces was also a constant.

Joanne Misko Pierce—in the foreground in the dress—and Susan Malone Roley—partially visible near the back of group—were sworn in as the first two women FBI special agents in modern times, 1972. (Source: FBI.)

Controversies surrounding police excessive use of force began to surface, particularly after the infamous beating of Rodney King in Los Angeles in 1991. The question was raised whether the gender of the police officers had a correlation with the likelihood of the use of excessive force, and studies began to emerge. Most notably, the National Center for Women & Policing was formed in 1995 "to educate criminal justice policy makers, the media and the public about the impacts of increasing the representation of women in policing…ensuring that gender is always considered during the analysis of contemporary policing issues, and that law enforcement agencies strive for gender balancing their departments" and released a seminal study in 1999.

Police Use of Excessive Force: Taking Gender into Account

By the National Center for Women & Policing, a Division of the Feminist Majority Foundation
June 1999

The Feminist Majority Foundation and The National Center for Women & Policing have conducted extensive research, including a review of the literature and interviews with specialists nationwide on women in policing and police violence. The research has profound implications for this Conference's work in examining and proposing solutions to the problem of excessive police violence. Police excessive use of force is costly to communities—in lives lost and damaged—and costly to taxpayers in money now paid out in settlements in police violence cases.

Research both in the United States and internationally shows that women police officers are less authoritarian and use force less often [than] their male counterparts, are better at defusing potentially violent confrontations, possess better communication skills, and respond more effectively to incidents of violence against women—a crime that accounts for as much as half the incoming calls to police departments.

Until now, the integration of women into the police agencies has been seen in terms of creating potential problems and costs. Policemen feared more women would compromise the department's toughness and competency, and thus lead to decreased morale. But after nearly 30 years of exhaustive research, the consensus of opinion is that women not only can do the job of policing equally as well as men, but in fact hold the key for substantially decreasing police violence and its cost to the taxpayer, while improving the ability of the police to respond to violence against women.

The full integration of women into policing is an opportunity for a constructive solution to the costly problems of police violence. These questions must be asked when examining the problem of police excessive use of force:

1. How do incidents of police abuse of force and citizen complaints break-down by gender and race of the police officer involved?
2. What is the break-down of the total monetary costs to the community and the severity of police violence by gender and race of the officer involved?
3. Is there a correlation between officers with domestic violence charges or complaints and excessive use of force complaints? Does the department track complaints of domestic violence, sexual assault and sexual harassment against male police officers? Are cases vigorously investigated?
4. Does the department screen recruits for personal views on the use of violence in gaining compliance and the use of violence within the family?

Studies on Police Use of Force by Gender

Research over the past three decades indicates that women police officers have a less authoritarian and aggressive policing style and use force less often than their male counterparts.

Lewis J. Sherman, in his research in the 1970s on women in policing, observed that "America's police forces remain bastions of male supremacy and American-style machismo," and he postulated that if more women were hired:

- Policewomen would precipitate less violence than policemen....
- By doing their jobs with less physical force, policewomen would do much to burnish the public's badly tarnished image of police officers.
- The less violent behavior of policewomen would spill over on policemen, who would learn that a decrease in muscularity often leads to an increase in efficiency.
- Policewomen would be considerably more effective than policemen in settling problems reported by women....

Sherman stressed that a greater number of women would lead to fewer violent confrontations between police officers and citizens: "The experiences of women in other hazardous work, the performance of police women in America and abroad, plus the social psychological research evidence all suggests that women tend to defuse volatile situations and provoke less hostility than men."

In an extensive review of the research on women in policing, Joseph Balkin reports that "policemen see police work as involving control through authority, while policewomen see it as a public service. The women's orientation is more likely to result in better relations with the public and a better image of police departments." Balkin went on to suggest that "...in some respects at least, women are better suited for police work than men...not all women are able to handle all police jobs—but neither are men."

Balkin concluded that although policemen continue to believe that "the women's relative lack of physical strength...could be a problem in dangerous and violent situations," the reality is that 80 to 95 percent of policing involves non-violent or service-oriented activities. And in defense of policewomen, Balkin points out in his review of the research in this area:

> ...physical strength has never been shown to be related to police functioning (Sherman 1973). No research has shown that strength is related to an individual's ability to manage successfully a dangerous situation (Bell 1982). There are no reports in the literature of bad outcomes because a policewoman did not have enough strength or aggression (Charles 1981)...Lehtinen (1976) observed that the ability to defuse a potentially violent situation is preferable to the use of strength. Rogers (1987) argued that coolness and skill are more important than strength in conflict situations.

An expansive 1974 study by Peter Bloch and Deborah Anderson sponsored by the Police Foundation concluded that introducing a substantial number of women officers would positively impact police operations:

> A department with a substantial number of policewomen may be less aggressive than one with only men. Women act less aggressively and they believe in less aggression. The presence of women may stimulate increased attention to the ways of avoiding violence and cooling violent situations without resorting to the use of force.

The men and women studied for this report performed patrol work in a generally similar manner. They responded to similar types of calls for police service while on patrol and encountered similar proportions of citizens who were dangerous, angry, upset, drunk or violent. According to the study, there was no difference in the number of injuries between male/female patrol teams.... In fact, the study found that the female officer is more likely than a male officer to calm a potentially violent situation and avoid injury to all of the participants. Chief Oliver Thompson of the Inglewood Police Department testified that "if I had my druthers, I would hire a greater number...of women officers than I would of men officers because of the less[er] number of citizen complaints...confrontations, the less[er] number of challenges that you have out there in the field."

Studies in the 1980s and early 1990s, have shown women to be more effective in many facets of the policing discipline: Women police officers rely less on violence and more on verbal skills in handling altercations, they are less likely to be involved in "serious unbecoming conduct," and they are more effective in handling female victims of violence.

In his 1983 study of the performance of women in the Los Angeles Police Department, Kenneth Hickman made similar findings. Hickman noted that women had superior communication skills, field tactics, initiative and self-confidence, and were more adept at public relations. The 1990 Claremont Graduate School study on the selection, recruitment, training, appointment and performance of women and minorities found that "females on probation were the subject of significantly fewer citizen complaints than either male or minority officers."

The Christopher Commission, which studied use of force in the Los Angeles Police Department in 1991, stated:

> Virtually every indicator examined by the commission establishes that female LAPD officers are involved in excessive use of force at rates substantially below those of male officers. There were no female officers among the 120 officers with the most use of force reports.

The Christopher Commission also looked at the top 10% of the LAPD officers ranked by the combined use of force reports, personnel complaints and officer-involved shootings and determined:

> There were no female officers among the top 132 officers. Only 3.7% of the 808 LAPD officers with the highest number of incidents were female officers. The statistics indicate that female officers are not reluctant to use force, but they are not nearly as likely to be involved in use of excessive force.... Many officers, both male and female, believe female officers are less personally challenged by defiant suspects and feel less need to deal with defiance with immediate force or confrontational language.

Studies show that because of their less authoritarian personalities, there is less likelihood of escalation of potentially violent situations with women police officers than with men. Researcher Carol Ann Martin found that "Women have proven that they have excellent communication skills which can be extremely helpful in police-citizen encounters where there may be potential violence. Quite often if the male officer is of the John Wayne-type he will provoke a fight or violence, instead of calming down the situation."

In sum, adding equal numbers of women police officers will reduce incidents of police violence and enhance the ability of police agencies to modify their policing styles in line with societal needs and realities. The lack of women police officers reinforces and exaggerates the authoritarian and traditional personalities which thrive on violence. Composed of people who have a common background and a common set of social attitudes and values, police departments reflect a "male fraternity" where unacceptable behavior not only receives little peer scrutiny but is actually reinforced by other members of the group.

Beyond Tokenism: The Need for Gender Balance

Since its inception in early 1995, the National Center for Women & Policing has been a leading force behind increasing the numbers of women in policing. The positive impact of women in policing, including the reduction of police brutality, increased efficacy in police response to domestic violence, and the increased emphasis on conflict resolution over force, mandates that we strive for gender balance in policing.

Yet, our research shows that the increase of women in law enforcement remains stuck at an alarmingly slow rate. Women comprise only 13.8% of all sworn law enforcement positions nationwide—a paltry increase of one-half of one percent from 1997 and only 3.2 percentage points from 1990 when women made up 10.6% of officers.

The data are clear: at the present rate of growth, women will not achieve equality in law enforcement agencies for several generations. Furthermore, the data shows that there has been progress only when women law enforcement officers and women's organizations have taken legal action to fight the discriminatory hiring and promotion practices and when court ordered consent decrees have forced agencies to increase the numbers of women or minorities hired and promoted.

The full integration of women into law enforcement departments must be seen as an opportunity, and policewomen themselves can only be seen as an asset to policing. Simply stated, the integration of women into law enforcement is a solution to the costly problem of police violence.

The goal must be a police force that reflects the community's entire population. But in order to increase the numbers of women in police departments across all police functions, it will be necessary to have formal plans and administrative structures for mandated change and gender balance.

Experts emphasize the need to create a "formal administrative structure" established specifically to achieve social equity for women in policing. Susan Martin, in *Women on the Move*, recommends police departments:

- concentrate voluntary affirmative action efforts on enlarging the pool of women recruits
- alter promotional standards to eliminate criteria that are irrelevant to supervisory ability or potential
- adopt stringent policies for dealing with sexual harassment
- alter work conditions [for] increasing the number of women in recruitment training and assignments
- periodically monitor departments to ensure that women are not tracked into clerical (or "female") assignments.

Penny Harrington of the Portland Police Department became the first female police chief in the country in 1985. (Randy L. Rasmussen/*The Oregonian*.)

In 1994, Beverly Harvard of the Atlanta Police Department became the first African American woman police chief in the United States. (Source: U.S. Department of Justice.)

To this must be added: alter hiring requirements to eliminate criteria that are irrelevant to performance and thus are non-job related. That is, to hire more women, police departments must overcome the serious problem that police work is still "perceived as a male oriented profession with a major emphasis on physical strength."

Conclusion

This Conference should call on law enforcement agencies nationwide—federal, state, and local—to move rapidly in achieving equal numbers of women and men and racial parity in their ranks if police violence is to be reduced. We must again call attention to the lack of real progress over the past 20 years in bringing women into policing in significant numbers. Clearly, what has been done historically to integrate police departments is inadequate and is costing Americans a high price—in human suffering and taxpayer dollars.

The National Center for Women & Policing added valuable statistics and advocacy to the conversation of policewomen. Unfortunately, they experienced lack of funding in the mid-2010s and have since closed. Their website with links to relevant publications remains active, however.

The second half of the twentieth century allowed great strides in advancing the policewoman's place on the force. Hiring statistics were up, as were training opportunities, and the first female police chief in America—Penny Harrington in Portland, Oregon—was appointed in 1985. In 1994 Beverly J. Harvard was appointed chief of police in Atlanta, Georgia, becoming America's first African American female police chief. But as the movement passed its centennial, there was still much work to be done. Certain stigmas still shaded people's views of policewomen's ability to perform, and equality was still a long way off.

Chapter 7

Modern Policewomen and Contemporary Concerns

Just as the late twentieth century brought landmarks for women in police, the 2000s have as well. In 2004 the first Asian American woman to become a police chief was Heather Fong, in San Francisco, California. Canadian Margaret Shorter became president of the IAWP in 2013. Portland, Oregon, hit the headlines again with the appointment of African American Danielle Outlaw as chief of police in 2017. And across the country, we are seeing more women from other underrepresented communities joining police forces and climbing the ranks as well.

Heather Fong of the San Francisco Police Department was the first Asian American woman police chief in 2004. (Courtesy of San Francisco Police Department.)

Danielle Outlaw, chief of Portland police as of 2017. (Reproduced by permission of the City of Portland.)

It's also a time when honest evaluation of effective practices and equal hiring practices is of critical concern, and the Police Foundation endeavors to address it head-on and work for a solution.

The 2000s and Beyond
Police Foundation, 2016

Many of the Police Foundation's early areas of emphasis have been continued and advanced over the years, and most themes generated during our first 40 years are still relevant today. Among them are the increased emphasis on police legitimacy, accountability, professionalization, and safety of the police; practices to prevent, control, and improve crime investigations; the growing need for data and technology to increase efficiency and effectiveness; as well as a focus on victims of crime, terrorism, and homeland security, as well as personnel strategies and officer safety. The present and future goals of the Police Foundation emphasize organizational learning through examination of near misses, organizational errors, and sentinel events. We have also returned to our roots in managing civil disorders, personnel management and safety, and investigative excellence. We have begun to focus on how public policy and advanced technology has an impact on and will continue to have an impact on communities and the police, as well as the growing need for evidence on what works in policing....

Moving Forward With Police Legitimacy, Accountability, and Community Policing
In the project report, *The Abuse of Police Authority*, the Police Foundation published the results of the first truly representative national survey of how America's rank-and-file police officers and their supervisors view critical issues of abuse of police authority.

Police legitimacy is fundamental to police effectiveness. Research has shown that when the public views the police as legitimate, they are more likely to obey the law, comply rather than challenge an officer's request, and assist police by providing information and participating in community crime prevention efforts. To that end, the Police Foundation works with municipal officials, police agencies, non-governmental organizations, and communities to create the constructive change necessary for improved police–community partnerships and delivery of services. For example, projects in Omaha, Nebraska, and Inglewood, California, were designed to facilitate collaboration among police and community leaders. Another project examined both the organizational culture of a police department, as well as community perceptions of that department, in an effort to build community trust and promote police accountability.

Another geographically based study conducted by the Police Foundation in Seattle showed that when supervisors have routine meetings with officers to discuss incidents using procedural justice, there is some impact on discretionary arrests and use of force (they go down)....

To address the rising tide in assaults on police officers and gun violence more broadly, the Police Foundation joined with nine other national law enforcement organizations to create the National Law Enforcement Partnership to Prevent Gun Violence, a collaboration committed to addressing the problems of gun crime and violence. These ten organizations—Commission on Accreditation for Law Enforcement Agencies, Hispanic American Police Command Officers Association, International Association of Campus Law Enforcement Administrators, International Association of Chiefs of Police, Major Cities Chiefs Association, National Association of Women Law Enforcement Executives, National Organization of Black Law Enforcement Executives, National Sheriffs' Association, Police Executive Research Forum, and Police Foundation—believe that law enforcement can play a unique and essential role in educating policy makers and citizens on the realities of gun violence in the communities they serve and in developing common-sense, data-driven solutions to reduce firearm-related injuries and deaths from homicides, suicides, and accidental shootings.

To confront the dilemma facing so many local police agencies about how to balance civil rights protections, community-policing priorities, and immigration enforcement, the Police Foundation launched a national project that brought together law enforcement executives, policy makers, elected officials, scholars, and community representatives in a series of focus groups across the country and at a national conference in Washington, DC. Attendees collaboratively examined the implications on local law enforcement of immigration laws and found that most law enforcement executives found a conflict in balancing the need for victims to report crime and others to cooperate in solving crime, while also enforcing federal immigration law, except in cases of felonies. The Police Foundation presented its 256-page report, *The Role [of] Local Police: Striking a Balance Between Immigration Enforcement and Civil Liberties*, to Congress in May 2009. It has participated in a series of meetings at the White House and Department of Homeland Security (DHS) on enforcement of federal immigration law by police. The report has served as a catalyst to examine policy and practice and underscore the complex balance that law enforcement agencies need to strike as they maintain their community-policing philosophies.

In early 2015, the Police Foundation became the first national policing organization to engage in the open data movement, leveraging open data's transparency and accountability features to help in restoring trust and confidence in law enforcement agencies in America. The Police Foundation proactively developed and launched the Public Safety Open Data Portal, which currently features calls for service, incident, arrest, stops, and use of force data from more than 20 law enforcement agencies from around the country which have agreed to make full and complete data sets available in a machine-readable format for anyone to access and use. The Portal provides consolidated access to the data and provides context and explanation to help users understand law enforcement data and its limitations. The Police Foundation is also playing a key role in supporting the White House's Police Data Initiative (PDI), an initiative designed to encourage the use of open data in policing.

Interestingly, the Police Foundation does not mention policewomen's role in reducing violence, despite the fact that this outlook has gained more and more traction throughout the discussion on use of force by police. Civil rights activist and prolific writer Shaun King makes the case in the *Daily News* that "at every phase of life, men are more violent than women.... We need so many reforms for law enforcement in America, but hiring hundreds of thousands of women to lead and guide these departments should jump to the very top of the list."

In 2010 the Women's Justice Center took a hard look at why there aren't more women on police forces.

Breaking and Entering the Thick Blue Line—Where Is the Women's Movement?
Women's Justice Center, 2010

Having exhausted judicial avenues to try and save her career, ex-police officer Debra Hartley is exasperated, tired, and miffed; but she's nowhere near giving up! On July 3, 2009, she set out on foot from her home in northern Pennsylvania to walk 225 miles to the White House. Debra couldn't win justice for herself, so she's trekking the distance to spotlight the rampant sex discrimination in law enforcement that dooms the careers of so many other good female police officers, and robs our communities of the immense benefits women bring to policing....

Two decades of research makes clear, female officers have dramatically lower rates of excessive use of force and citizen complaints than do male officers. Female officers are also better at de-escalating volatile situations, at handling cases of violence against women, and in carrying out the goals of community policing. In short, female officers overall bring with them exactly the improvements that so many communities across the country say they are seeking in their police forces....

Yet despite the proven benefits, and despite the fact that ever more women are entering policing, the nationwide percentage of women in policing is actually going down, from a mere 14% females in the year 2000 to 12% today. The pattern is disheartening. Women get hired on, chewed up, and spit out in what Debra Hartley so aptly refers to as "the revolving door". Studies also provide a window on the problem. The number one on-the-job stress for female officers, studies show, is not the criminals, nor the rigors of the work. It's the attitudes of the male officers.

It's Not Working Anywhere

Here on the west coast, frustrated by years of our own attempts to increase the number of women in our local Sonoma County police departments, we cheer Debra on. For the last 15 years, we have gathered statistics, launched over a dozen lawsuits, put together task forces, made the rounds of city councils meetings, organized protests, gathered thousands of signatures, flown in police experts from across the country, held town hall meetings...and look!

By our most recent tally in November, 2008, out of a total of 666 officers on our ten local police forces here in progressive Sonoma County, there are only 8% female officers, a mere couple of percentage points gain since starting our push 15 years ago. Worse, there are only a total of 7 female officers in the ten departments who hold the rank of sergeant or above. Worst of all, as of the same November tally, only five percent of the upcoming cadets in our local police academy are female.

Whether going at it from the inside, as Debra Hartley and so many other female officers have done, or hammering at it from the outside, as we have, it's not working. If anything, male control of police powers in our country is being consolidated.

So Here Are a Couple of Our Thoughts as to Why It's Not Working and What We All Can Do About It

Most people make a gross underestimation of the force needed to bring about change in law enforcement. Unlike many other professions that have seen a slow, but steady, softening of barriers, and corresponding gains for women, law enforcement has remained an insular haven of hyper male culture trending more toward digging in their heels and galvanizing forces to drive women out. A revealing 2003 study by the National Center for Women in Policing found that the major gains for women in policing often come only under court ordered consent decrees resulting from lawsuits.

Most disturbingly, the study further found that once the time period of those decrees has lapsed, there is a swift erosion of progress and a rapid wholesale loss of female officers.

The details of individual women officers' lawsuits add to this picture, showing time and again that the top brass, right up to the chiefs, are often actively involved in driving women out. Once a [woman] complains about discrimination, male officers often join together up the ranks in retaliating against her. There is also a sickening, but very common pattern of perpetrator officers being promoted rather than being punished. Much as it happened in Debra's case.

This entrenched unwillingness of police to change with the times and open the doors, despite a steady barrage of lawsuits, means a whole lot more pressure needs to be coming from the outside—and not just in a couple of counties....

So Where Is the Women's Movement?

The women's movement, most notably the violence-against-women arm of the women's movement, has been conspicuously absent from the fight. In fact, it's shown a decided antipathy for the task. There are a couple noteworthy exceptions. The National Center for Women in Policing, for example, in the late 1990's and early 2000's was making monumental strides to promote women in policing. But even their efforts have waned in recent years.

There are any number of reasons why women's groups have shied away from this fight, some more obvious than others. The willingness of police to abuse their enormous powers to retaliate against any group that challenges their status quo is well known—and daunting. Indeed, police agencies have succeeded in crushing a number of women's crisis centers that dared to criticize law enforcement practices. Unless a group is seriously focused on the task, with strategy and resources sufficient to match the inevitable powerful police back-attacks, not too many organizations can withstand the blows.

Another reason there is so little focus on increasing the number of women in policing is that people in general, including women's groups, don't realize just how critical improved, non-sexist policing is to obtaining women's freedom. The women's movement has done a phenomenal job of passing a full spectrum of legislation to deal with violence against women. But there's a hugely mistaken belief that once a law is passed, police automatically have to enforce it. The reality is that police have enormous discretionary powers in deciding which crimes to treat seriously and which to ignore.

The reality is, despite police rhetoric, their sexism in enforcement decisions prevails. Far too many police choose to ignore, disregard, under-investigate, and, in any other of a hundred ways, blow off victims of violence against women, and blow off the laws that were passed to protect women. If police can't even work with female officers, imagine how they treat the victims of violence against women, especially when it's up to the individual officer's discretion.

With rigidly male dominated police forces standing as the arbitrary gatekeepers to so many women's safety, justice, and freedom, breaking up this patriarchal stronghold should be at the top of women's agendas.

Follow the Money

But alas, there is one other little discussed, but significant reason that the women's movement has neglected this critical task. To understand it, one need only heed the maxim, "follow the money[.]"

In 1994, when the federal Violence Against Women Act infused the system with big money, as so often happens, it all came with some sinister strings attached. In the beginning, in order to obtain a share of this money, rape and domestic violence centers in most states had to show evidence of their cooperation with their local law enforcement. Usually this was carried out by requiring that the women's centers obtain signatures from their local police chiefs and DA's on a "memorandum of understanding" between the law enforcement agency and the women's center.

And, voila! Just that fast, police and district attorneys had effective veto power over the violence-against-women movement's core funding. All police had to do was refuse to sign, or threaten to refuse to sign[,] or put conditions on signing, and women's centers either fell in line or they fell. Since then, things have only gone from bad to worse.

Over the last 15 years, rape and domestic violence centers have become increasingly entangled in contractual relationships with law enforcement; such as having advocates' offices in the police department, obtaining grants together, interweaving all manner of policies, programs, and finances. Along with some obvious benefits for victims, the downside has been just as predictable. The U.S. violence against women movement has become increasingly embedded in the very institutions we most need to change. The feminist rape and domestic violence centers of yesterday have become morphed into the quasi governmental service agencies of today. The leading edge of the struggle to change law enforcement and end violence against women has been blunted. The once vibrant feminist violence-against-women movement has been reduced to endlessly mopping up the human debris left in the patriarchy's wake.

It's All Doable

The tasks ahead for fully integrating women into law enforcement are fairly clear and they're all do-able. Police sex/race statistics need to be monitored up into the ranks and down into the academies—and publicized. Police recruitment tactics need to be challenged, as do hiring, retention, and promotion practices. Communities need to be educated to the importance and benefits of women in policing. Other social justice and police watchdog groups need to be joined in the task. Women activists have to revamp their toolboxes. And individual female officers have to be supported.

It is all do-able. But, before any of it can make real headway, we need to re-invent an independent, feminist, violence-against-women movement that can stand the fight. This doesn't mean dismantling the service organizations we have now. But it does mean directing considerable effort to fomenting independent women's groups to the task.

We also need a women's movement overall that puts the goal of increasing women in law enforcement on their national agendas. Police power and culture are too powerful and galvanized for individual groups to succeed in isolated efforts. But even igniting a national focus on the issue is unlikely to happen unless the violence-against-women movement takes the lead.

Meanwhile, too many women's pleas for help are being met by hostile, sexist police officers who know they can turn their backs and get away with it. And ex-police officer Debra Hartley, who we desperately need back on the job, is walking alone to the White House. "I'm hoping that doing something remarkable like this[,]" says Debra, "We can draw enough attention to this problem, and get people talking and involved, and get enough media interest in the issue, to get some policies changed."

Clearly, Debra Hartley cannot, and should not, be doing it alone. ❧

Although this kind of discrimination was a strong concern in 2010, some police chiefs had already begun to place it front and center in their initiatives for bettering police forces.

Policewomen: Their First Century and the New Era

By Peter Horne

The Police Chief, September 2006

Promoting Progress for Women in Policing

In 1998, to promote progress of women in policing, the International Association of Chiefs of Police

(IACP) created an ad hoc committee on women in policing. The committee, composed of female law enforcement executives throughout the United States, was directed to examine the role of women in policing and to report its findings to the IACP Board of Officers. The study, The Future of Women in Policing: Mandates for Action, was published in November 1998. The survey of 800 IACP members revealed or confirmed critical information regarding the status and future of women in policing.

The IACP survey reported results similar to those of the survey conducted by the NCWP: policewomen are both underused and undervalued in law enforcement. While confirming that the number of women in policing is growing and progressing through the ranks, it also revealed the following:

- There are few women in policing, compared to their male counterparts.
- Female officers still face bias from male officers.
- Many departments lack strategies for recruiting women.
- Female officers may face gender discrimination and a so-called "brass ceiling" that inhibits promotion.
- Sexual harassment still occurs in many departments.
- There are few mentoring programs for female officers.

Women Make Valuable Contributions to Community Policing

As the 1998 IACP report noted and the current statistics confirm, significant barriers still confront women in policing. Yet, despite the pessimistic views of some regarding the future of policewomen, there is much to be optimistic about during these early years of the 21st century. A number of legal and cultural obstacles to women in policing have been removed. There are signs that things are beginning to improve, and that women considering a career in law enforcement today may not have to experience all the hardships that confronted their predecessors.

Community policing was the buzzword in police circles during the 1990s. Many departments around the country became community policing departments or adopted parts of community policing. While police administrators and others have different definitions of the term, community policing is essentially a department-wide philosophy and management approach that promotes community, government, and police partnerships and proactive problem solving to address crime, fear of crime, social and physical disorder, and quality of life. It shifts the focus of police work from handling random calls to solving ongoing community problems.

Even in this post–September 11 era, there are a number of indications that community policing will survive in the 21st century, and that it is more than a passing fad. The growing emphasis on community policing demands police officers with problem-solving and communication skills that enable them to interact effectively with all segments of the public. Several researchers have noted that women tend to be effective communicators, and they also are good at solving problems. Hiring policewomen (or more policewomen), retaining them, and promoting them will help police departments succeed in community policing.

Can Policewomen Improve Police Response to Female Victims?

One segment of the community that has received increased attention from the police is female victims of violence. Although the specific numbers vary widely, it is safe to conclude that violence against women (including domestic violence and rape) is a significant problem in the United States. Nationwide, an estimated 2 million women are severely assaulted by male partners each year. Some 1,500 of them die. The police have estimated that more than 40 percent of all calls for police service are in some way related to domestic violence.

Domestic violence is probably the most common form of violence today. It is important to note that most violent crimes against women go unreported. In the past, it has been estimated that less than 10 percent of domestic violence incidents were reported to the police. Female victims of domestic violence are sometimes reluctant to call the police because they believe that officers will not help or that the officers will side with the male perpetrator of the violence.

It has been suggested that increasing the number of policewomen handling complaints of domestic violence would dramatically enhance a police department's ability to respond effectively to violence against women. Studies have shown that female police officers believed more strongly (than male officers) in the need to show sympathy and understanding to successfully handle domestic disputes. A 1985 study portrayed policewomen as being more involved in domestic violence calls and more convinced (than male officers) of the importance of responding to family fights as a crucial police duty. Increasing the number of women in policing at all ranks and in all operational capacities would improve the handling of domestic violence and sexual assault cases. It would also encourage female victims of violence to report such incidents to the police because they will be more confident that their pleas for help will be treated seriously.

Policewomen Are Less Likely to Use Excessive Force

Regarding violence, it is essential to note that numerous studies have shown that policewomen rely on a policing style that uses less physical force and is less confrontational than that used by many policemen. Policewomen are much less likely to use excessive violence or police brutality while satisfactorily performing their jobs. In the aftermath of the infamous 1991 beating of Rodney King in Los Angeles, the Independent Commission (Christopher Commission) on the Los Angeles Police Department issued a report that included the following: "Female officers utilize a style of policing that minimizes the use of excessive force. Data examined by the Commission indicate that LAPD female officers are involved in use of excessive force at rates substantially below those of male officers." It concluded that pervasive gender bias contributed substantially to excessive-force problems on the LAPD.

Police agencies around the country have lost lawsuits often involving large sums of money to settle excessive force suits brought by citizens, yet a number of reports in the past 25 years in the United States and abroad show that the less confrontational approach to policing used by the majority of female officers and some male officers results in more effective law enforcement and less use of force. Police departments can substantially reduce their exposure to excessive force lawsuits if more women are employed as police officers and used in all facets of policing and in all ranks as well.

The Mass Media and Policewomen

The mass media has put a positive spin on the portrayal of policewomen in the last 15 years or so. Today the print media does not run the sensational front-page stories about the first policewoman hired or promoted. Articles about women in policing are more matter-of-fact or routine these days.

Early television serials about female police officers in the 1970s, *Get Christie Love* and *Police Woman*, focused on female undercover and plainclothes officers. But starting with *Cagney and Lacey* in the mid-1980s and continuing with such shows as *Hill Street Blues*, *NYPDBlue*, *ThirdWatch*, *Law and Order: SVU*, and the various CSI shows, female detectives and uniformed officers are portrayed as competent, valuable members of the police force, and other characters treat their presence as unexceptional. The ascendance of women in police dramas is unequivocal and pretty much television-wide. It has occurred in movies as well. The media attention has helped promote favorable attitudes toward female officers among the general public, prospective police candidates, and even police officers themselves.

Changing Attitudes

Attitudes concerning policewomen have changed for the better, and the media has contributed to this. It has been found that there is a growing acceptance by the public for females in the law enforcement role. Especially noteworthy is that most people are no longer skeptical of women's ability to handle violent situations.

Today, more than two-thirds of male criminal justice students are supportive of female officers overall and, of course, a good number of these students will be going onto careers in policing where they may well be working with female colleagues. It is now not uncommon for male police officers to acknowledge that women make good cops. And a number of larger and midsize police agencies are actively recruiting, employing, and promoting more women.

Policewomen Find Networking and Support in Associations

A number of state, regional, national, and international associations have emerged to give support to female officers and give an organized voice to the interests of policewomen. The oldest national association is the International Association of Women Police (IAWP). This association was formed in 1956 as a continuation of the International Association of Policewomen (IAP), which was founded in 1915 by Alice Wells and others and discontinued during the Depression in 1932. Today it has approximately 3,000 members.

Three other organizations promoting women in policing arose in the 1990s. The National Association of Women Law Enforcement Executives (NAWLEE), started in 1995, has some 400 voting members at the rank of lieutenant or above in their respective departments. The National Center for Women and Policing (NCWP), also organized in 1995, has several hundred members. The NCWP produces and disseminates research on issues relevant to women in law enforcement. A fourth national association for U.S. policewomen, Women in Federal Law Enforcement (WIFLE), was reorganized and renamed as WIFLE in June 1999. It also has several hundred members.

These organizations provide information, guidance, and support to female officers and those considering entering the profession. These four associations have sought to educate police administrators, politicians, the media, and the public about the benefits of increasing the number of women in policing.

Forcing Change

Female candidates and officers continue to file discrimination lawsuits, and they are forcing changes in police agencies. These lawsuits sometimes result in court-ordered consent decrees that require agencies to change their policies. A consent decree is an agreement between parties (instead of a final decision by a judge) that binds a police department to a particular course of action in regard to hiring and promoting women in law enforcement. Female officers have filed gender discrimination and sexual harassment lawsuits as well, and a majority of these have been settled in favor of the complainant (the policewoman). But many of the women who file these suits face retaliation and even ostracism from their police departments. In an ideal world these lawsuits would not be necessary, but the women who challenge the system today are forcing change that will ultimately benefit the women (and men) who enter policing tomorrow.

The history of women in policing is nearing the time when there will be no more "firsts." Many police agencies have already experienced the first woman hired, the first woman to be promoted to whatever rank, the first woman on the SWAT team, the first woman commander, and so on. Unfortunately, the first women in these cases have often experienced added scrutiny as they did their jobs. They paid a price for opening up doors for future women to pass through. Some of these female pioneers advanced in policing while others did not survive in their careers. But they all helped break down barriers in large and small law enforcement agencies at all levels of government.

It would be very easy for someone to be pessimistic about the future of women in policing. The percentage of policewomen is still relatively small and the rate of increase of policewomen has grown at a snail's pace since 1971. Unfortunately, as the NCWP points out, court-ordered plans still remain necessary to get some police agencies to implement policies to recruit, promote, and retain women. Two major barriers still exist in many police departments: sexual harassment and poor maternity leave policies.

The Next Generation

Women have made steady, albeit modest, strides in law enforcement since the 1970s. As of the end of 2002, an estimated 17 percent of recruits who completed police academy training (throughout the nation's police academies) were female. Many police agencies have taken action to eliminate or reduce employment barriers and improve working conditions.

Women have a 125-year history of police work and currently make up about 12 percent of U.S. police forces. (©kali9/iStockphoto.)

The IACP has gone on record stating that it "believes it is essential to strengthen the position of women in policing-their numbers, their professional development, their progress to positions of leadership, and their contribution to the public service and safety."

It is also noteworthy that Chief MaryAnn Viverette's presidency of the IACP in 2005–2006 is occurring as policewomen close out their first century in U.S. policing. It is interesting that this is occurring while the first generation of women officers in the modern era (started in 1972) is retiring and the second generation is coming on board police agencies. The female baby-boomer officers who were hired by police agencies in the 1970s and early 1980s now have more than 25 years of service and either have retired or will be retiring in the next few years. In case there are still lingering doubts in anyone's mind, the efforts of these women have improved law enforcement and paved the way for even greater contributions by the next generation of women police officers.

As Horne points out, much of the reason we don't see equal numbers of women as men on police forces is because of the sexist environment women report working in, and this was still true eleven years after Horne's article, when the Pew Research Center released a telling survey.

Female Police Officers' On-the-Job Experiences Diverge from Those of Male Officers

By Renee Stepler

Pew Research Center, January 17, 2017

...The nationwide survey of 7,917 police officers in departments with at least 100 officers finds that many female officers think men in their department are treated better than women when it comes to assignments and promotions. About four-in-ten female officers (43%) say this is the case, compared with just 6% of male officers. By contrast, a third of male officers say women are treated better than men when it comes to assignments and promotions in their department—but just 6% of women say this is the case. Six-in-ten male officers and half of female officers say men and women are treated about the same.

When it comes to their experiences in the field, women are less likely than men to say they have physically struggled with a suspect who was resisting arrest in the past month (22% vs. 35% of male officers). Six-in-ten female officers say they have been verbally abused by a citizen while on duty in the past month, compared with 69% of men. These differences remain when looking only at officers currently on field assignments, such as a patrol officers and detectives. Most police (72%) say they have *never* fired their weapon while on duty outside of required training or on a gun range. Female officers are much less likely than male officers to report that they have ever fired their weapon while on duty—11% of women vs. 30% of men.

There is also a significant gender gap in attitudes on policing, with female officers less likely than their male counterparts to agree that aggressive tactics are sometimes necessary. Among female officers, 48% agree that it is more useful to be aggressive than to be courteous in certain parts of the city, compared with 58% of male officers. A third of female officers—but 46% of male officers—agree that some people can only be brought to reason the hard, physical way....

As slowly as the statistics of policewomen and the attitudes of police in general are shifting, change is happening. We see this domestically as women like MaryAnn Viverette and Danielle Outlaw take leadership roles in their communities and our nation. And in 2015, three policewomen in Portland, Oregon, responded to a little girl in Camas, Washington, who thought that only boys could be police. They took a photo posing with a sign that read, “Girl cops are awesome!” which made local news. We can hope that increased numbers of policewomen from all walks of life will become more visible and inspire girls of the younger generation to consider becoming policewomen.

And just as we’re seeing more and more women proudly take their place on police forces in America, the same is true in other countries. Many have employed policewomen for as long as, or perhaps even longer than, America, while others are relatively new to the movement. The following headlines give a taste of the role of policewomen worldwide:

- “10 Outstanding Policewomen of PH [Philippines] Feted,” Inquirer.Net, October 12, 2016
- “Palestinian Police Take New Steps to Widen Career Opportunities for Women in the Police,” UNISPAL, February 24, 2017
- “Tasmanian Policewomen Celebrate 100 Years in the Force with an Eye on the Top Job,” *ABC News, Australia,* March 7, 2017
- “Team Building for Police Women Held in Belize City,” *Breaking Belize News,* March 17, 2017
- “India’s Ladycops,” *Aljazeera,* March 30, 2017
- “In Afghanistan, an Elite Female Police Officer Battles Cultural Taboos as well as the Taliban,” *Los Angeles Times,* May 3, 2017

With the upward trend of the policewomen movement as we advance further into the twenty-first century, we can hope for a brighter, more peaceful future worldwide.

Conclusion

The Gift of Policewomen traces the work of policewomen from the last years of the nineteenth century, through the twentieth century, and into the twenty-first. While several other books have been written on the movement, for most of the twentieth century, writers cast two early policewomen as combatants for the title of the first policewoman. When records of a third female police officer revealed service dates even earlier than the other two, the previous conclusions were destroyed. *The Gift of Policewomen* reveals the backgrounds of all three—Marie Connolly Owens, Lola Greene Baldwin, and Alice Stebbins Wells—and accepts them as a trio of pioneers for the policewomen movement.

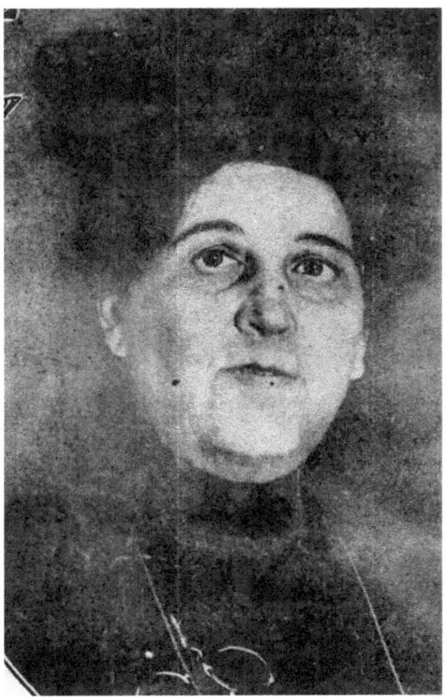

Of the histories that do cover the pioneers, most tend to jump from their service early in the movement to the 1970s, when feminism started to bring more women to police forces. However, there were many other trailblazing policewomen in the intervening years. In short, about sixty years of police history has been sadly ignored. *The Gift of Policewomen* has attempted to shine a light on these women as well and tell a fuller history. Sadly, not every policewoman in the history of the movement can be listed in a book with a finite number of pages. I have endeavored to include the main landmarks in the movement and the women who were behind them, and I hope the reader will forgive any omissions.

Currently, women make up about 12 percent of American police forces, and yet the history of policewomen demonstrates that women are extremely competent officers. Furthermore, studies show they are much less likely to lapse into excessive use of force or neglect safety protocols, truly representing the goal to protect and serve. It's time for police forces nationwide—even worldwide—to implement a goal for 50 percent representation and strategies to both recruit women and combat the sexism they experience in police departments. It will take more strong leadership from policewomen as well as active effort from policemen to foster an environment where all police officers can thrive. And it will benefit policewomen, policemen, and the public immeasurably.

The policewomen movement of the past 125 years has featured many strong, inspirational women who have made history. I never would have known about them had it not been for my grandmother, Assistant Superintendent Wilma Crounse, and the research that her career led me to undertake. *The Gift of Policewomen* is a salute to her, the thousands of policewomen who have served to date, and the many more who are to come.

Acknowledgments

Originally, my goal for this project was to chronicle my grandmother's life and how she came to join the Portland Police Department in the early 1900s. This part of my research appeared to be a cinch. I was in the possession of a number of family treasures that had trickled down over time until I inherited them. But though I had much to work with, there was also much I didn't know, and this became even more clear as the project grew to include so many more policewomen within a national and international movement. I contacted many libraries and other resources ranging from East Coast to West, and I am deeply indebted to the following libraries, historical societies, records collections, and individuals for the records they shared:

Ancestry.com
Architectural Heritage Center in Portland, Oregon, especially Val Ballestrem
City of Portland, Oregon: Archives & Records Management, especially Mary B. Hansen
Douglas County Historical Society in Roseburg, Oregon, especially Peggy A. Rowe-Snyder
Forest Grove City Library in Forest Grove, Oregon, especially Ismoon Hunter-Morton
Friends of Historic Forest Grove in Forest Grove, Oregon, especially Mary Jo Morelli
The Genealogy Center at Allen County Public Library in Fort Wayne, Indiana
GenWeb of Monroe County, New York, especially Dick Halsey
Graceland Cemetery in Chicago, Illinois, especially Saifa T. H.
The Huntington Library Manuscripts Collection in San Marino, California, especially Robert Maine
Monroe County Library System in Rochester, New York, especially Dick Halsey
Multnomah County Central Library in Portland, Oregon
Nebraska State Historical Society Library in Lincoln, Nebraska, especially Nancy Drake and Cindy S. Drake
NewsLibrary.com
North Springfield Baptist Church Library in North Springfield, Vermont, especially Pastor George Keeler
Oregon Historical Society in Portland, Oregon, especially Hannah Allan

Oregon Secretary of State: Vital Records Listings
Pacific University Library Archives in Forest Grove, Oregon
PdxHistory.com
Portland Police Museum and Historical Society in Portland, Oregon, especially Liza Dormandy, Jim Huff, and Wayne Kuechler
State Historical Society of Iowa in Des Moines, Iowa, especially Sharon Avery
Washington State University Libraries, Manuscript, Archives, and Special Collections in Pullman, Washington
Watzek Library Special Collections and Archives, Lewis & Clark College in Portland, Oregon

I'd also like to thank these people for their valuable assistance, support, and encouragement in this project: Kay Derochie, who jump-started me; Ali Shaw, my thoughtful and patient editor; my family, Kevin Ullman, Neal Ullman, and Arlene Ullman; and Mike Moorad, Gertrude Marian (Brice) Drake, Bertha Lee Crounse, and Dorothy M. Lewis.

Bibliography

Abbott, Edith. "Training for the Policewomen's Job." *Woman Citizen*, April 1926.

Adameisenberg.com. "A Different Shade of Blue: How Women Changed the Face of Police Work." Press materials. Accessed June 18, 2018. http://www.adameisenberg.com/a-different-shade-of-blue/.

Akron Beacon Journal Staff. "Akron Policewoman Battled Vice and Crime in 1930s and 1940s." *Akron Beacon Journal*, March 23, 2008. https://www.ohio.com/akron/lifestyle/akron-policewoman-battled-vice-and-crime-in-1930s-and-1940s.

Al Jazeera. "India's Ladycops." March 30, 2017. https://www.aljazeera.com/programmes/specialseries/2017/03/india-ladycops-170328121136978.html.

American City. "The Police-Woman Is Marching On." November 1913, 403. https://books.google.com/books?id=S4Q3AQAAMAAJ&pg=RA1-PA403&dq.

Bakken, Gordon Moris, and Brenda Farrington, eds. "Wells, Alice Stebbins (1873–1957)." In *Encyclopedia of Women in the American West*, 286. Thousand Oaks, CA: Sage, 2003. https://books.google.com/books?id=E0g5DQAAQBAJ&pg=PA286&lpg=PA286&dq.

Baldwin, Lola. Travelers' Aid Funding Request, letter to Mayor Harry Lane. December 1, 1907.

BBN Staff. "Team Building for Police Women Held in Belize City." *Breaking Belize News*, March 17, 2017. https://www.breakingbelizenews.com/2017/03/17/team-building-police-women-held-belize-city/.

Brandenburger, John A. "Effective Work of Policewomen." *American City*, March 1923, 259–60. https://archive.org/stream/americancity28granrich#page/260/mode/2up.

Brownlow, Louis. "The City Manager and the Policewoman." *Woman Citizen*, November 1925.

Buwalda, Imra Wann. "The Policewoman Yesterday, Today and Tomorrow." *Journal of Social Hygiene* 31, no. 5 (May 1945). 290–93. https://archive.org/stream/journalofsocialh31amerrich/journalofsocialh31amerrich_djvu.txt.

———. "Policewomen on the Pacific Coast." *Woman Citizen*, March 1927.

Charity Organization Society of the City of New York. "Western Women as Police Officers." *Survey*, December 21, 1912, 345–47. https://books.google.com/books?id=MvBQAQAAMAAJ&pg=PA346&lpg=PA346&dq.

Chung, James. "A Canadian May Be America's First Female Cop." Hello Vancity, September 4, 2010. Updated November 14, 2010. http://www.hellovancity.com/news/a-canadian-may-be-americas-first-female-cop/.

Clark, Jane Perry. "The Policewoman and Deportation." *Woman Citizen*, June 1927.

Connolly, Vera. "Job for a Lady: Detroit's Police-Women Apply Humane Values to the Girl-Delinquency Problem." *Collier's Weekly*, June 10, 1944: 18–19. http://www.unz.com/print/Colliers-1944jun10-00018/.

Corbett, Gertrude P. "Society News." *Morning Oregonian*, January 7, 1915. https://oregonnews.uoregon.edu/lccn/sn83025138/1915-01-07/ed-1/seq-8.

———. "Society News." *Morning Oregonian*, March 20, 1915. https://oregonnews.uoregon.edu/lccn/sn83025138/1915-03-20/ed-1/seq-10.

Dame, Lawrence C. "Portland Police Progress—Past and Present: An Authentic Historical Sketch," as submitted by Virginia Gronborg of the Maine Historical Society, August 8, 1978.

Darwin, Maud. "Policewomen: Their Work in America." *Nineteenth Century and After* 75 (June 1914): 1371–77. https://books.google.com/books?id=6FVDAQAAMAAJ&pg=PA1371&dq.

Davis, Katharine Bement. "The Police Woman." *Woman Citizen*, May 30, 1925.

De Jesus, Julianne Love. "10 Outstanding Policewomen of PH [Philippines] Feted." Inquirer.Net, October 12, 2016. http://newsinfo.inquirer.net/824550/10-outstanding-policewomen-of-the-philippines-for-2016-feted.

Drusus, Livius. "Marie Connolly Owens, America's First Female Police Officer." Mental Floss, January 21, 2017. http://mentalfloss.com/article/62534/marie-connolly-owens-americas-first-female-police-officer.

Engel, Robin Shepard. "Police: History." *Encyclopedia of Crime and Justice*. Last modified June 16, 2018. Accessed June 18, 2018. https://www.encyclopedia.com/law/legal-and-political-magazines/police-history.

"Expanding Role of Women in Police Service." *Journal of Criminal Law and Criminology* 36, no. 5 (January–February 1946): 332. https://www.jstor.org/stable/1138045.

Faizy, Sultan. "In Afghanistan, an Elite Female Police Officer Battles Cultural Taboos as well as the Taliban." *Los Angeles Times*, May 3, 2017. http://www.latimes.com/world/la-fg-afghanistan-female-police-2017-story.html.

Harris, Mary B. "The Socialized Policewoman." *Woman Citizen*, June 27, 1925.

Higgins, Lois. "Historical Background of Policewomen's Service." *Journal of Criminal Law and Criminology* 41, no. 6 (1951). https://scholarlycommons.law.northwestern.edu/cgi/viewconten .cgi?article=3865&context=jclc.

Hodder, Jessie D. "Police—Before or After?" *Woman Citizen*, January 1926.

Holloway, Maryann. "The World's Outstanding Women (WOW): Alice Stebbins Wells." *If I Only Had a Time Machine* (blog), September 13, 2014. https://mholloway63.wordpress.com/2014/09/13 /the-worlds-outstanding-women-wow-alice-stebbins-wells/.

Holmes, Edith Knight. "Women's Clubs." *Morning Oregonian*, December 17, 1916. https://oregonnews .uoregon.edu/lccn/sn83045782/1916-12-17/ed-1/seq-52.

Horne, Peter. "Policewomen: Their First Century and the New Era." *The Police Chief* 73, no. 9 (September 2006): 56–58, 60–61. http://www.iawp.org/history/policewomenfirstcentury.htm.

Hutzel, Eleanore L. "The Policewoman." *ANNALS of the American Academy of Social and Political Science* 146, no. 1 (November 1, 1929): 104–14. http://journals.sagepub.com/doi /pdf/10.1177/000271622914600110.

International Association of Women Police. "History of the IAWP." Accessed June 18, 2018. http://www .iawp.org/history/historyoftheIAWP.htm.

———. "The IAWP Past & Present." Accessed June 18, 2018. http://www.iawp.org/history/pastpresent.htm.

Janik, Erika. "From Mothers to Crime Fighters." Chap. 9 in *Pistols and Petticoats: 175 Years of Lady Detectives in Fact and Fiction*. Boston: Beacon Press, 2017. https://books.google.com /books?id=8kIdDgAAQBAJ&pg=PA153&lpg=PA153&dq.

King, Shaun. "To Combat Police Brutality, Hire More Female Cops—Studies Show They're Better at Keeping Their Cool." *Daily News*, August 3, 2016. http://www.nydailynews.com/news/national /king-combat-police-brutality-hire-female-cops-article-1.2737314.

Kluckhohn, Florence R. "American Women and American Values." In *Cold War in the Nuclear Age*, 159–62. Vol. 17 of *The Annals of America 1950–1960*. New York: Encyclopædia Britannica, 1968.

Literary Digest. "A 'Mother' of Disillusioned Girls in New York City." March 15, 1924.

Literary Digest. "Policewomen in Chicago." August 23, 1913. https://books.google.com /books?id=rQw8AQAAMAAJ&pg=PA271&lpg=PA271&dq.

Literary Digest. "The Policewomen of Indianapolis and Their New Methods." April 23, 1921. https://archive .org/stream/literarydigest69newy#page/n282/mode/1up.

Martin, Susan Ehrlich, and Nancy C. Junik. *Doing Justice, Doing Gender: Women in Legal and Criminal Justice Occupations.* Thousand Oaks, CA: Sage, 2006. https://books.google.com/books?id=89mlq7AIIsoC&pg=PT67&lpg=PT67&dq.

McGroarty, John Steven. *California of the South*, Vol. 5. Chicago: S. J. Clarke, 1933.

Meares, Hadley. "Meet 'Deadshot Mary,' a 1930s Undercover Cop Superstar." *Atlas Obscura*, May 25, 2016. https://www.atlasobscura.com/articles/meet-deadshot-mary-new-york-citys-1930s-undercover-cop-superstar.

Michigan Women's Hall of Fame. "Eleonore Hutzel (1885–1979)." Accessed June 18, 2018. http://www.michiganwomenshalloffame.org/Images/Hutzel,%20Eleonore.pdf.

Moorad, Elizabeth S., and Wilma Crounse. "Lola G. Baldwin." In *With Her Own Wings: Historical Sketches, Reminiscences, and Anecdotes of Oregon's Pioneer Women*, edited by Helen Krebs Smith. Rockville, MD: Wildside Press, 2008. https://books.google.com/books?id=jQoRjPEVOO0C&pg=PA232&lpg=PA232&dq.

Morning Oregonian. "Bathing Suits Worn by Girls Approved: Censors Find One Abbreviated Costume Too Immodest, but Mermaid Ignores Plea: Moral Effects Studied." June 30, 1915. https://oregonnews.uoregon.edu/lccn/sn83025138/1915-06-30/ed-1/seq-13.

Morning Oregonian. "Care of Refugees: Portland Women Keep Up the Good Work." April 27, 1906. https://oregonnews.uoregon.edu/lccn/sn83025138/1906-04-27/ed-1/seq-13.

Morning Oregonian. "Fair Auto Driver's Traffic Signal Misses Its Mark." October 7, 1915. https://oregonnews.uoregon.edu/lccn/sn83025138/1915-10-07/ed-1/seq-7.

Morning Oregonian. "For Travelers' Aid: Association Discusses Means of Continuance: What the Reports Show." October 20, 1905. https://oregonnews.uoregon.edu/lccn/sn83025138/1905-10-20/ed-1/seq-14.

Morning Oregonian. "Lost Kelso Girl Is Found: Freda Lyon, 16 Years Old, Is Domestic in St. Helen's Hall." September 14, 1911. https://oregonnews.uoregon.edu/lccn/sn83025138/1911-09-14/ed-1/seq-7.

Morning Oregonian. "Some Places Where Christmas Cheer Is Needed." December 22, 1905. https://oregonnews.uoregon.edu/lccn/sn83025138/1905-12-22/ed-1/seq-13.

Morning Oregonian. "Woman Is Good Shot: Mrs. Wilma Crounse Shows Policemen How to Use Revolvers." January 24, 1918. https://oregonnews.uoregon.edu/lccn/sn83025138/1918-01-24/ed-1/seq-5.

Moss, Margaret. "If I Were a Policewoman." *Woman Citizen*, October 1925.

Murray, Virginia M. "Policewomen in Detroit." *American City*, September 1921, 209–10. https://books.google.com/books?id=ZLBCAQAAMAAJ&pg=PA209&lpg=PA209&dq.

National Center for Women & Policing. "About Us." Accessed June 18, 2018. http://womenandpolicing.com/aboutus.asp.

———. "A History of Women in Policing." Accessed June 18, 2018. http://womenandpolicing.com/history/historytext.htm.

———. "Police Use of Excessive Force: Taking Gender into Account." June 1999. Accessed June 18, 2018. http://womenandpolicing.com/kstestimon.html.

Nelson, Josephine. "On the Policewoman's 'Beat.'" *Independent Woman*, May 1936.

New World Encyclopedia. "Gabriel Tarde." Last modified May 17, 2017. Accessed June 18, 2018. http://www.newworldencyclopedia.org/entry/Gabriel_Tarde.

O'Grady, Ellen A. "Policewomen and Their Work." *American City*, January 1919, 59–60. https://books.google.com/books?id=q7tEAQAAIAAJ&pg=PA59&lpg=PA59&dq.

Oregon Daily Journal. "College Girls Will Serve in This Hotel." April 23, 1905. https://oregonnews.uoregon.edu/lccn/sn85042444/1905-04-23/ed-1/seq-6.

Oregon Daily Journal. "Protection of Girls Object of Society." March 7, 1905. https://oregonnews.uoregon.edu/lccn/sn85042444/1905-03-07/ed-1/seq-2.

Oregon Daily Journal. "Women Unite to Save Womankind." April 16, 1905. https://oregonnews.uoregon.edu/lccn/sn85042444/1905-04-16/ed-1/seq-13.

Owens, Marie. "Enforcement of the Child Labor Law: Twelve Years Detective Sergeant Detailed to Board of Education on This Work." *Chicago Tribune*, July 28, 1901. https://chicagology.com/chicagopolice/marieowens/.

Owings, Chloe. "Author's Note." *Women Police: A Study of the Development and Status of the Women Police Movement*. New York: Frederick H. Hitchcock, 1925. https://babel.hathitrust.org/cgi/pt?id=uc1.$b269197;view=1up;seq=10.

Parker, Valeria H. "A Policewoman's Life." *Woman Citizen*, June 28, 1924.

Paul, Catherine A. "National Child Labor Committee (NCLC): Founded April 25, 1904." 2017. Accessed June 18, 2018. http://www.socialwelfarehistory.com/organizations/national-child-labor-committee.

Pigeon, Helen D. "From the Diary of a Policewoman." *Woman Citizen*, December 1925.

———. "From the Diary of a Policewoman—II." *Woman Citizen*, June 1926.

———. "One Thousand Sponsors." *Woman Citizen*, May 1927.

———. "The Policewoman's Due." *Woman Citizen*, August 1926.

Police Foundation. "The 2000s and Beyond." Last modified 2016. Accessed June 18, 2018. https://www.policefoundation.org/about/history/recent-history/.

———. "History of the Police Foundation." Last modified 2016. Accessed June 18, 2018. https://www.policefoundation.org/about/history/.

Shine, Rhiannon. "Tasmanian Policewomen Celebrate 100 Years in the Force with an Eye on the Top Job." *ABC News, Australia*, March 7, 2017. http://www.abc.net.au/news/2017-03-08/female-police-celebrate-gains-in-tasmania/8335426.

Smith, Betsy Brantner. "Police History: The Evolution of Women in American Law Enforcement." PoliceOne, June 30, 2015. https://www.policeone.com/police-history/articles/8634189-Police-History-The-evolution-of-women-in-American-law-enforcement/.

Steenberg, Edward J. "Ed." "Our Matrons & Police Women." Saint Paul Police Historical Society. Accessed June 18, 2018. www.spphs.com/history/matrons.php.

Stepler, Renee. "Female Police Officers' On-the-Job Experiences Diverge from Those of Male Officers." Pew Research Center, January 17, 2017. http://www.pewresearch.org/fact-tank/2017/01/17/female-police-officers-on-the-job-experiences-diverge-from-those-of-male-officers/.

Sunday Oregonian. "Issues a Warning: Women Should Not Come to Seek Work: No Field for the Unskilled." March 12, 1905. https://oregonnews.uoregon.edu/lccn/sn83045782/1905-03-12/ed-1/seq-16.

Survey. "Police Women's Efficiency in Danger." May 2, 1914, 110. https://books.google.com/books?id=37pIAAAAYAAJ&pg=PA110&dq.

Topping, Ruth. "Counselors-at-Large." *Woman Citizen*, April 1927.

UN Women. "Palestinian Police Take New Steps to Widen Career Opportunities for Women in the Police." UNISPAL, February 24, 2017. http://palestine.unwomen.org/en/news-and-events/stories/2017/02/police-women-career.

Van Winkle, Mina C. "Policewomen in Conference." *Woman Citizen*, August 8, 1925.

Wells, Alice Stebbens [*sic*]. "Women on the Police Force." *American City*, April 1913, 401. https://books.google.com/books?id=p5VEAQAAIAAJ&pg=PA401&lpg=PA401&dq.

Wells, Sandra K., and Betty L. Alt. *Police Women: Life with the Badge*. Westport, CT: Praeger, 2005. https://books.google.com/books?id=Bd1GbzIr270C&pg=PA8&dq.

Wilson, O. W., and Roy Clinton McLaren. "Public and Community Relations." *Police Administration*. New York: McGraw-Hill, 1977.

Winter, Alice Ames. "The Policewoman of Policewomen." *Ladies' Home Journal*, July 1927.

Women's Justice Center. "Breaking and Entering the Thick Blue Line—Where Is the Women's Movement?" 2010. http://justicewomen.com/pw_whereisthewomensmovement.html.

Special Credits

The following publishers and rights holders granted special permission to reprint pieces featured in this book. This page constitutes an extension of the copyright page.

Copyright © Marie De Santis, Women's Justice Center, www.justicewomen.com, rdjustice@monitor.net: Women's Justice Center. "Breaking and Entering the Thick Blue Line—Where Is the Women's Movement?" 2010. http://justicewomen.com/pw_whereisthewomensmovement.html.

Encyclopedia of Crime and Justice, V3, 2E. © 2002 Gale, a part of Cengage, Inc. Reproduced by permission. www.cengage.com/permissions: Engel, Robin Shepard. "Police: History." *Encyclopedia of Crime and Justice*. Last modified June 16, 2018.

Excerpt reprinted with permission from Pew Research Center: Stepler, Renee. "Female Police Officers' On-the-Job Experiences Diverge from Those of Male Officers." Pew Research Center, January 17, 2017. http://www.pewresearch.org/fact-tank/2017/01/17/female-police-officers-on-the-job-experiences-diverge-from-those-of-male-officers/.

Originally published in Ladies' Home Journal® magazine, July, 1927. Used with permission from Meredith Corporation: Winter, Alice Ames. "The Policewoman of Policewomen." *Ladies' Home Journal*, July 1927.

Quote by Adam Eisenberg, courtesy of http://www.adameisenberg.com/a-different-shade-of-blue/: Adameisenberg.com. "A Different Shade of Blue: How Women Changed the Face of Police Work." Press materials.

Reprinted by permission of the National Center for Women & Policing © 2001:

National Center for Women & Policing. "About Us." http://womenandpolicing.com/aboutus.asp.

———. "A History of Women in Policing." http://womenandpolicing.com/history/historytext.htm. Reprinted by permission of the National Center for Women & Policing.

———. "Police Use of Excessive Force: Taking Gender into Account." June 1999. http://womenandpolicing.com/kstestimon.html. Reprinted by permission of the National Center for Women & Policing © 2001.

Reprinted by special permission of Northwestern University School of Law, *The Journal of Criminal Law and Criminology*: "Expanding Role of Women in Police Service." *Journal of Criminal Law and Criminology* 36, no. 5 (January–February 1946): 332. https://www.jstor.org/stable/1138045.

Reprinted from *The Police Chief* (September 2006). Copyright held by the International Association of Chiefs of Police, Alexandria, VA. Used with permission: Horne, Peter. "Policewomen: Their First Century and the New Era." *The Police Chief* 73, no. 9 (September 2006): 56–58, 60–61.

Reprinted with permission of the *Akron Beacon Journal* and Ohio.com: Akron Beacon Journal Staff. "Akron Policewoman Battled Vice and Crime in 1930s and 1940s." *Akron Beacon Journal*, March 23, 2008.

Reprinted with permission of the Police Foundation:

Police Foundation. "The 2000s and Beyond." Last modified 2016. Accessed June 18, 2018. https://www.policefoundation.org/about/history/recent-history/.

———. "History of the Police Foundation." Last modified 2016. Accessed June 18, 2018. https://www.policefoundation.org/about/history/.

This article abides by terms of the Creative Commons CC-by-sa 3.0 License (CC-by-sa), which may be used and disseminated with proper attribution: *New World Encyclopedia*. "Gabriel Tarde." Last modified May 17, 2017. http://www.newworldencyclopedia.org/entry/Gabriel_Tarde.

Used with permission from International Association of Women Police (IAWP®):

Abbott, Edith. "Training for the Policewomen's Job." *Woman Citizen*, April 1926.

Brownlow, Louis. "The City Manager and the Policewoman." *Woman Citizen*, November 1925.

Buwalda, Imra Wann. "Policewomen on the Pacific Coast." *Woman Citizen*, March 1927.

Clark, Jane Perry. "The Policewoman and Deportation." *Woman Citizen*, June 1927.

Davis, Katharine Bement. "The Police Woman." *Woman Citizen*, May 30, 1925.

Harris, Mary B. "The Socialized Policewoman." *Woman Citizen*, June 27, 1925.

Hodder, Jessie D. "Police—Before or After?" *Woman Citizen*, January 1926.

International Association of Women Police. "History of the IAWP." http://www.iawp.org/history/historyoftheIAWP.htm.

———. "The IAWP Past & Present." http://www.iawp.org/history/pastpresent.htm.

Moss, Margaret. "If I Were a Policewoman." *Woman Citizen*, October 1925.

Parker, Valeria H. "A Policewoman's Life." *Woman Citizen*, June 28, 1924.

Pigeon, Helen D. "From the Diary of a Policewoman." *Woman Citizen*, December 1925.

———. "From the Diary of a Policewoman—II." *Woman Citizen*, June 1926.

———. "One Thousand Sponsors." *Woman Citizen*, May 1927.

———. "The Policewoman's Due." *Woman Citizen*, August 1926.

Topping, Ruth. "Counselors-at-Large." *Woman Citizen*, April 1927.

Van Winkle, Mina C. "Policewomen in Conference." *Woman Citizen*, August 8, 1925.

Used with permission from Michigan Women Forward—HERstory: Michigan Women's Hall of Fame. "Eleonore Hutzel (1885–1979)." http://www.michiganwomenshalloffame.org/Images/Hutzel,%20 Eleonore.pdf.

Used with permission from the publisher: Connolly, Vera. "Job for a Lady: Detroit's Police-Women Apply Humane Values to the Girl-Delinquency Problem." *Collier's Weekly*, June 10, 1944: 18–19. http://www.unz.com/print/Colliers-1944jun10-00018/.

Used with permission from the publisher: Meares, Hadley. "Meet 'Deadshot Mary,' a 1930s Undercover Cop Superstar." *Atlas Obscura*, May 25, 2016.

Used with permission of PoliceOne: Smith, Betsy Brantner. "Police History: The Evolution of Women in American Law Enforcement." PoliceOne, June 30, 2015. https://www.policeone.com/police-history/articles/8634189-Police-History-The-evolution-of-women-in-American-law-enforcement/.

Cover Images:

New York Policewomen: *Police Women - Capt. Edyth Totten and women police reserve. New York City.* Photograph. Retrieved from the Library of Congress, <www.loc.gov/item/2006675559/>.

Mabel Kruse: Courtesy Bobbi Harmon.

Lola Baldwin: Oregon Historical Society, #bb014193.

Alice Stebbins Wells: Courtesy Los Angeles Police Museum.

Marie Owens: *Chicago Sun Tribune,* August 7, 1904.

Mary Shanley: *Mary Agnes Shanley, New York City detective, full-length portrait, facing slightly right.* Photograph. Retrieved from the Library of Congress, <www.loc.gov/item/2004676750/>.

Lucy Grey and Aletha Gilbert: Courtesy Los Angeles Police Museum.

Index

Page numbers in *italics* refer to illustrations.

About the Author

Robert Neal Ullman has lived most of his life in Oregon. With a master's of teaching degree from Portland State University, he taught eighth-grade social studies and coached cross-country and track for twenty-six years. In 1985 he was a semifinalist in Oregon for the Teacher in Space Project. He and his family also lived in Pinchbeck, England, for a year, where he taught on a Fulbright Teacher Exchange.

Mr. Ullman has done extensive research on his family tree and has had several articles published in the *Oregonian* regarding genealogy. After years of research and interviews on women in the field of police work, this is his first published book.

Mr. Ullman has two sons, two daughters-in-law, and one granddaughter. He lives with his wife in beautiful Central Oregon.

CPSIA information can be obtained
at www.ICGtesting.com
Printed in the USA
BVHW080531171118
532724BV00007B/13/P

9 780578 40303